spiritual practices

for effective LEADERSHIP

7 Rs of SANCTUARY for Pastors

DEBORA JACKSON

FOREWORD BY LOVETT H. WEEMS JR.

JUDSON PRESS
PUBLISHERS SINCE 1824

VALLEY FORGE, PA

Spiritual Practices for Effective Leadership: 7 Rs of Sanctuary for Pastors
© 2015 by Debora Jackson
All rights reserved.

Interior design by Crystal Devine.
Cover design by Wendy Ronga and Hampton Design Group.

Library of Congress Cataloging-in-Publication Data

Jackson, Debora.
  Spiritual practices for effective leadership : 7Rs of sanctuary for pastors / Debora Jackson.
      pages cm
  ISBN 978-0-8170-1758-3 (paperwork : alk. paper) 1. Christian leadership. 2. Pastoral theology. I. Title.
  BV652.1.J323 2015
  248.8'92--dc23
                              2014025828

Printed in the U.S.A.

First printing, 2015.

contents

Foreword   v
Acknowledgments   ix

Part One   Introduction   1
Chapter 1   Leadership and Efficacy   7
Chapter 2   Time Apart   25
Chapter 3   Spirituality and Spiritual Praçtices   39

Part Two   Introducing the 7 Rs of Sanctuary   53
Chapter 4   Retreat   59
Chapter 5   Release   71
Chapter 6   Review   85
Chapter 7   Reconnect   99
Chapter 8   Reflect   117
Chapter 9   Recalibrate   135
Chapter 10   Return   151

foreword

"WHEN THE PAIN Outweighs the Promise" is the poignant title of an article on poor morale among spiritual leaders that drew my attention several years ago. That title describes the urgent need for a book such as *Spiritual Practices for Effective Leadership: 7 Rs of Sanctuary for Pastors* by Debora Jackson. To attend to the life of the spirit is the foundation for leadership in the church. It has always been so.

Richard Baxter's classic on pastoral ministry, *The Reformed Pastor*, first published in 1656, makes it clear that spiritual leaders must always take care of themselves spiritually before they can offer help to anyone else. He cautioned pastors not to famish themselves while preparing food for others. By "reformed" Baxter refers not to a doctrinal stance, but rather to "renewal"—the renewed pastor.

A renewed and more effective ministry is precisely Jackson's goal. She encourages spiritual leaders to take time away and observe spiritual practices not only for their own sakes, but so they can return to their ministry contexts "refreshed and ready to re-engage in the work" to which they are called.

This book comes at a critical time. Church leaders feel stuck. They are trapped in ways of leading that are out of sync with the circumstances they encounter. Their frustration comes not so much from the heavy workload, though it is immense, but from the futility of trying to use skills and methods that no longer bear fruit. The complexity and rapidity of change today requires much more than the acquisition of more skills; it requires nothing less than a new way of thinking. It requires what Paul called for in Romans to be "transformed by the renewal of your minds." It is from such renewed ways of thinking that we are able to discern God's will and be the leaders God would have us be.

Today the challenge is to help leaders renew their minds to meet ever-changing circumstances. There may have been a time when the acquisition of basic knowledge and a set of specialized skills would serve someone for a long time, but this is not such a time. The new leader must be far more adaptable to changing circumstances. Today's leaders will need to be much more comfortable with ambiguity in order to be always looking for clues and patterns in the changing landscape. Effective church leadership in this era will involve incomplete solutions, much trial and error, and a great deal of learning.

As outlined in Jackson's book, the pattern of retreat for renewal and reentry with new energy and insights makes such ongoing learning and adaptation possible. Innovation is the challenge of our time, and innovation does not come from working harder. It comes from such steps as those proposed by Debora Jackson in this timely book.

Jackson addresses this challenge out of her personal experience of a health crisis. That crisis led to research and reflection on what is required for spiritual leaders to remain effective over the long term. The author draws upon Ronald Heifetz's concept of sanctuary as a mental or physical haven that permits reflection and renewal. However, she adds the dimension of spiritual practices to Heifetz's definition in order to give it more specificity and to fit more appropriately for church leaders.

She develops her 7 Rs of Sanctuary:

- Retreat
- Release
- Review
- Reconnect
- Reflect
- Recalibrate
- Return

These steps are developed with real-life illustrations from actual spiritual leaders so that readers can adapt them for their own personalities and circumstances. In addition to leading to better emotional, mental, and spiritual health, these practices make effective and fruitful leadership much more likely. They make it more likely as well that God can continue to work the "renewal of our minds" so necessary for leadership.

All pastoral leaders will identify with the dilemma Jackson so carefully describes, and we will benefit from her experience and insights. Whether one is new to church leadership or is a long-serving leader, the lessons will be timely.

LOVETT H. WEEMS JR.

Distinguished Professor of Church Leadership

Director of the Lewis Center for Church Leadership

Wesley Theological Seminary, Washington, DC

Author with Tom Berlin of *Bearing Fruit: Ministry with Real Results*

acknowledgments

TO GOD BE the glory. I am so grateful to God for the divine unction on my life. It is a blessed privilege to share the wisdom that God has entrusted to me. I praise you, Lord. I thank God for my parents, Theodore and Carolyn Jackson. You cheer me on; you help me stand. You are constant sources of strength and love. Thank you for always being there for me.

To my co-researchers, I remember you with admiration and appreciation as I read your stories embedded in these pages. Your names are hidden, but I will never forget for they are written on my heart.

To my editor, Rebecca Irwin-Diehl: from our first conversation, you saw the potential of this work and have labored with me through this entire project to its completion. I appreciate you.

To friends and colleagues who have supported me in this process, prayed for me throughout, and offered words of encouragement along the way, I could never name you all, but I am grateful for you.

To Earl Walker, Teresa Walker, and Danielle Walker of Image360 in Tucker, Georgia, thank you for designing my 7 Rs of Sanctuary graphic. It so perfectly speaks to the power of this process.

To my husband, my love, James Thomas, thank you for your love and support. And to our son, Jadon Theodore Thomas, the light of my eyes: truly what I do, I do for you.

✦ PART ONE ✦

introduction

ARE PASTORS WHO intentionally take time to engage in spiritual practices more effective in their ministry leadership? This is the question that inspired me to write this book. Wanting to help pastors become their best selves as they balance the challenges and demands of leadership, I developed the 7 Rs of Sanctuary—a process designed to help pastors realize effectiveness in leadership while contributing to their spiritual wholeness and well-being. Not only is the aforementioned question my personal passion, it is also a critical issue in pastoral leadership.

Generally, the work of leadership is increasingly complex. I have had the privilege of leading organizations in a variety of environments: for-profit, nonprofit, religious, and secular. The goals of each organization varied from maximizing shareholder wealth to leading souls to Christ. Yet—regardless of the context—I have learned the challenges that leaders confront remain the same. Leaders are expected to achieve goals and objectives that deliver tangible results while balancing numerous variables often beyond the control of any individual.

Pastors must understand that the expectations for ministry leadership are much the same: realize tangible results in the form of growing the congregation, encouraging membership, and implementing ministries that foster deepening spiritual life. However, achieving such goals, especially as societal values about church and organized religion change, is impossible for a pastor to accomplish alone. Instead, it is increasingly incumbent upon pastors to motivate and mobilize others in the community of faith to understand the challenges, learn from those challenges, and then apply the lessons learned to advance the work of the local church.

Such ministry leadership is made all the more challenging when the community views the church as a volunteer organization. With aging members and dwindling church membership, how do pastors motivate people to engage in the work? How do they lead effectively given increasingly complex environments?

In addition, the work of leadership work requires a continuously evaluative capacity to review the work of the ministry and seek opportunities for improvement. What was effective twenty years ago in church is less effective now. Therefore, congregations must constantly review their methods to seek new ways to increase each local church's impact on its community. And pastoral leaders must provide oversight to this process and cycle to determine whether the current model for ministry is effective. This practice of review and evaluation must become the standard way of operating. It is the pastor's work to inspire this generative capacity where the congregation is continuously learning and seeking ways to apply new ideas with renewed energy, even as challenges arise.

Yet, how does a pastor do this intentional work most efficaciously?

The complexity of these and other challenges make it easy for a pastor to lose perspective. It certainly happened to me as pastor—I was an ex-officio member of each church board and committee by virtue of my role as pastor. However, time after time when I attended these meetings, I found myself taking on a major leadership role in the meetings. Even worse, I would leave those meetings shouldering responsibility for the majority of the action items the group had identified.

I was so busy doing the *work* of the boards and committees that there was no time left for me to do the work of the pastorate. I was writing sermons in the middle of the night and responding to emails during what should have been family time, while the strategic work of leading the church had virtually ceased. In the end, I suffered a health crisis; the stress of how I was working became unbearable. Something had to change.

Often, pastors engage in the thick of situations and, as a result, may lose their way. Rather than leading with vision, the pastor may become mired in details, unable to inspire creativity. Such a loss of perspective can lead to depletion and stress.

I have witnessed this in pastors who experience signs of burnout, who have hit a proverbial wall in their ministries, finding themselves unable to think or focus. I have seen pastors fall into ministry maintenance mode, with dwindling energy spent trying to hold the institution together rather than lead the community with passion. I have observed pastors who suffer depression as they withdraw from situations and people, unable to meaningfully engage.

Yet, the situation can grow more dire. The stresses of leadership and the challenges it brings may so overwhelm some pastors that they become physically unwell, experiencing headaches, upset stomach, elevated blood pressure, insomnia, and chest pain.

Having experienced many of these issues, I want more for ministry leaders today. I want pastors to become effective in mobilizing their congregations to solve new challenges in generative and dynamic ways, while at the same time learning as individual leaders to thrive in and not succumb to the challenges of leadership.

What are the practices or processes that will assist pastors in those goals? In his book *Leadership without Easy Answers*, Ronald Heifetz suggests that leaders in general need a strategy for deploying and restoring their spiritual resources; a practice that he calls creating sanctuary.[1] For Heifetz, sanctuary is the mental or physical haven to which one can intentionally retreat to create space for reflection and renewal. Sanctuary is a safe place removed from the demands of leadership and, so sheltered, offers the opportunity to consider challenges, learn lessons, and ultimately restore a sense of purpose. Thus defined, sanctuary can be recognized not only as an important leadership strategy, but also as the means by which leaders are able to regain perspective in the face of leadership challenges.

Of course, this begs the question, If Heifetz's concept of sanctuary provides such benefits, why aren't more leaders engaging in it?

One explanation I would offer is that the concept is not well-defined. Heifetz has consistently recommended this practice of creating sanctuary[2] as a means of enhancing and restoring one's spiritual resources. However, he avoids providing specific strategies about how to create sanctuary. Instead, Heifetz suggests that the specific details of creating sanctuary should be left to the individual. Without specific suggestions or instructions, the means by which one's spiritual resources are restored become difficult to determine. This shortcoming creates another obstacle to creating sanctuary. Lacking specific details on how to create sanctuary, the benefits also become difficult to identify.

Most people would concur that taking time away from our everyday existence is inherently beneficial, but they may also note that the benefits of doing so are difficult to quantify. Because tangible benefits cannot be readily recognized, the task of taking time apart may be reduced in importance as other priorities gain precedence. The sad result is that self-care practices such as creating sanctuary become casualties during times of mounting pressures.

Furthermore, being intentionally non-specific regarding the practice of creating sanctuary presents ambiguity. Heifetz speaks of restoring one's spiritual resources, but what exactly does this mean? Is this a religious or spiritual exercise? I believe the work can be viewed broadly as spirituality, in both religious and secular terms.

From a religious perspective, spirituality refers to "human interactions with the transcendent or divine."[3] It is the effort of seeking connection to that source beyond ourselves for guidance, clarity, or direction in order to renew our individual purpose. From a secular perspective, spirituality is the "desire to find ultimate purpose in life and to live accordingly."[4] It is the effort to realize self-actualization by finding our individual purpose and then engaging in those efforts that will enable each of us to live out that purpose.

Notice the commonality in the exercise of spirituality, and whether it is considered from a religious or secular viewpoint, the end result is the same. Through spiritual engagement, an individual can realize a renewed sense of purpose, which provides perspective about how that purpose fits in the greater context, and potential insight regarding how that purpose might be realized.

Thus, creating sanctuary is the joint effort of taking time apart and engaging in spiritual practices, and it is this effort that enables individual leaders to reengage their leadership contexts better prepared to mobilize others and inspire renewed creative, generative capacity in themselves. In short, all leaders emerge from my concept of sanctuary with the potential to lead more effectively.

If leaders can realize increased efficacy by taking time apart and engaging in spiritual practices, I contend that they might be more inclined to do so. This is especially true for pastoral leaders who are able to clearly recognize the benefit of engaging in spiritual practices.

NOTES

1. Ronald Heifetz, *Leadership without Easy Answers* (Cambridge, MA: The Belknap Press of Harvard University Press, 1994), 273.

2. The practice of creating or finding sanctuary is recommended in the books *Leadership without Easy Answers; Leadership on the Line: Staying Alive through the Dangers of Leading*, written with Marty Linsky; and *The Practice of Adaptive Leadership: Tools and Tactics for Changing your Organization and the World*, with Alexander Grashow and Marty Linsky.

3. Evan B. Howard, *The Brazos Introduction to Christian Spirituality* (Grand Rapids, MI: BrazosPress, 2008), 16.

4. Oliver F. Williams, ed., *Business, Religion, & Spirituality: A New Synthesis* (Notre Dame, IN: University of Notre Dame Press, 2003), 1.

·1·

leadership and efficacy

WHEN WE CONSIDER the importance of leadership, a consideration that consistently comes to the forefront is efficacy. What is efficacy in leadership? We inherently understand the importance of leadership, but what about efficacy? What is the relationship between leadership and efficacy? How may pastors realize efficacy in their pastoral leadership?

Leadership, which is the task of inspiring and mobilizing others to actively engage in the learning required to competently address the challenges that an organization faces,[1] is critical. But the work of leadership is focused on the *output* of the leader and of those whom he or she leads. Output is a measure of efficacy. More specifically, efficacy is the measure of that generative capacity within an organization or congregation to effectively cope with the demands, challenges, stressors, and opportunities it encounters[2] to maximize efforts.

Leadership influences this approach. "No matter what leaders set out to do . . . their success depends on *how* they do it."[3]

Leadership literature is filled with examples that connect leadership and efficacy. In their book *The Leadership Challenge*, leadership gurus and best-selling authors Jim Kouzes and Barry Posner speak of efficacy in terms of the work of a leader. Their study focuses on what the most effective leaders do when they were at their personal best.[4]

For Kouzes and Posner, efficacy is predicated on the actions of the leader. The most effective leaders will challenge the process. In terms of the pastorate, this means effective pastors will not simply retread old paths. These pastoral leaders want to ensure that what they do is optimal, and not simply revisiting what is habitual or traditional ("we've always done it this way").

Kouzes and Posner note that effective leaders inspire a shared vision. Certainly, pastors understand this. As Proverbs 29:18 says, "If people can't see what God is doing, they stumble all over themselves; But when they attend to what he reveals, they are most blessed."[5] By casting a vision, pastors motivate people to get on board to realize the vision.

Effective leaders also enable others to act. In the pastorate, this means pastors remove barriers so that people can succeed. Moreover, effective leaders model the way, setting the example for others as they progress through challenges. This ability to set an example is key in pastoral leadership because the pastor must be seen doing what he or she encourages others to do.

Finally, effective leaders encourage the heart. In the pastorate, such leaders recognize others' efforts, celebrate their achievements, and provide encouragement during moments of discouragement. When the pastor is operating at his or her best, showing the way for the congregation, the congregation can also be at its best.

From these examples, we see leadership and efficacy go hand-in-hand.

Kouzes and Posner are not the only authors who hold leaders chiefly responsible for efficacy. Max De Pree, a business professional and writer who is also an expert in the field of leadership, asserts that leaders are responsible for effectiveness. He explains that "efficiency is doing the thing right, but effectiveness is doing the right thing."[6]

De Pree is most concerned with helping leaders do the right things so they function at their best. This is an important distinction for pastoral leaders, as it is so easy for us to be caught in a trap of doing things right. We lead worship services, engage in mission programs, and encourage people to be involved with the work of the church. Yet, are these the right things to do?

If we find our services and programs are yielding diminishing returns, how then might we realize new opportunities? Too often, we go through the motions of reinstituting the same programs and people rather than examining the needs of our communities and responding in ways that invite new programs and new leaders to emerge.

This is the difference: we do not just want to do things right. We want to do the right things. This distinction is critical for De Pree because effectiveness, in his opinion, comes about through enabling others to reach their potential.[7]

Even for those who do not explicitly identify efficacy as an overriding concern, efficacy remains a prevalent concept. For example, Bill George, author and professor of management practice at Harvard Business School, contends in his book *True North* that the primary concern in leadership is authenticity. Pastoral leaders will understand this concern. We want people to see us as being authentic in our leadership. Yet, George notes that leaders can optimize effectiveness as they are able to empower people to lead around a shared purpose, thereby positioning an organization or congregation to achieve superior results.[8]

Jim Collins, author of *Good to Great*, sees the effective leader as less than the ultimate type of leader. Collins designates an Effective Leaders as a Level 4 leader, one who will catalyze commitment and pursues a clear and compelling vision to stimulate higher organizational performance.[9] Yet, such leadership does not inspire the "good to great" performance documented in Collins's study. Using the analogy of a fly wheel, Collins notes that we have to keep trying different things until something catches on.

This is a reality in pastoral ministry also, as we tinker with new ministries or different music during worship or a change in our outreach strategy. Notwithstanding, as institutions strive for greatness by applying the concepts identified in Collins's study and by eliminating unnecessary work efforts, those institutions are able to radically simplify their lives while increasing effectiveness.[10] Again, efficacy becomes a focus in leadership.

So, it seems that many management theorists relate efficacy with leadership, which is significant because numerous studies show a measurable correlation between leadership and efficacy. Scholar James G. Bohn demonstrates that people perceive leadership as the primary influencer of efficacy in terms of a sense of mission or purpose, a sense of collective capability, and a sense of resiliency.[11] Bohn went further to demonstrate statistical correlation between leadership and efficacy, showing that each of the following leadership behavioral qualities had a positive impact on efficacy:

✦ Leaders who know where they are going, thereby helping others feel confident about organizational direction;
✦ Leaders who maintain focus on goals, which instills organizational confidence;
✦ Leaders who have a credible track record of accomplishments;
✦ Leaders who can clearly communicate their ideas;
✦ Leaders who distinguish themselves as being able to get things done.[12]

These characteristics are in keeping with the expectations of the pastorate. Congregations look to their pastors to convey certainty, focus, and credibility. Pastors who are confident and clear about where they are going generate feelings of certainty in others. As a pastor maintains focus on goals and can clearly communicate that focus, he or she instills confidence.

A pastor will also garner an underlying element of trust based on previous accomplishments. People trust that past successes will lead to future successes and this creates credibility. People will confidently follow credible pastoral leaders. This level of trust and confidence also helps distinguish an effective pastor as a leader who can get things done.

Self-Differentiated, Emotionally Intelligent Leaders

These qualities place overwhelming pressure on the pastoral leader's ability to maximize the generative capacity of a congregation. It also begs the question, What does it take for a pastoral leader to be efficacious?

"To be determined, decisive, visionary and still keep your wits about you may be what it takes to reorient any marriage, family, organization, society or civilization,"[13] says rabbi and family systems theorist Edwin Friedman. For Friedman, these characteristics suggest that efficacy is realized when a leader has learned to face him or herself so that they are less likely to become lost in the anxious, emotional processes of others.[14] Friedman defines this as self-differentiation. It is a way of being—an internal, rather than external, orientation or focus. This notion of differentiation provides a new orientation for leadership.

Self-differentiation requires fortitude on the part of a pastoral leader. As pastors, our *effect* on our congregants has to do with the *affect* of our presence and being. Mature leadership, then, begins with the pastoral leader's capacity to take responsibility for his or her self and destiny.[15] According to Friedman, leaders need to focus on their personal integrity, presence, and being as a motivating orientation. This provides pastors with the capacity to gain clarity about their own purpose rather than focusing on strategies that center on others.

In addition, the individual must be able to exercise non-anxious leadership that is rooted in self-awareness. Clearly this is a necessary skill for pastoral leaders, as it is incumbent upon us to maintain a centered, grounded presence to create this same centeredness for others in the congregation. Anxiety among congregation members causes regression because it creates an emotional inability to move forward. Thus, a well-differentiated pastor's ability to resist anxiety and remain persistently focused on his or her vision will encourage others to do the same.

Pastoral leaders must also understand and see *self* beyond their role. Without this awareness, it is too easy to become caught up in the emotions of situations, particularly under threatening conditions, and become blind to the vulnerabilities that we do not wish to see in ourselves.[16] Through understanding self as separate from the role, pastors are able to appropriately disengage, assuming an objective view of the work rather than be subsumed by the congregational environment.

Mastering these capabilities is a challenge, as the focus of efficacy in leadership is not on helping the leader become well-differentiated. Most leadership studies see efficacy as rooted primarily in external factors, harnessed through efforts such as strategic planning or realizing increased productivity. As a result, leaders tend to focus on influencing such external factors as the means of maximizing efficacy. This is true in the pastorate as well. For example, we can be easily lured into the belief that if our boards or committees operated more effectively, then the church would flourish. Unfortunately, such a focus on external factors can backfire.

At issue is the fact that a system—be that system a family, society, or a congregation—values comfort over the rewards of facing challenges.[17] According to Friedman, systems seek to conform rather than confront. This can be particularly true in the church where many people view the worship experience as an opportunity to escape from the pressing challenges of daily life. We do not want our worship experience to be contentious. We do not want our worship experience to change. We want the worship experience of our childhood to prevail unchanged decades later. This is the epitome of conformity.

More than that, the issue is that these systems value a sense of togetherness that typically adapts to those who are least mature. When a common analogy for the church is a "hospital for sinners," we see the capacity to cater to the least mature. Because of this, such systems look for quick-fix solutions that temporarily alleviate symptoms without addressing fundamental problems. The culmination of such conformity for an organization is "a well-structured and natural 'funeral parlor'."[18] It is the choice of a slow death, demonstrating the preference for maintaining the status quo rather than dealing with the threat of facing change. Many churches are choosing that slow death rather than confronting change.

Friedman suggests such systems inhibit leadership because the immaturity of the system hinders if not cripples the capacity to be decisive.[19] In that state of indecision, systems seek comfort in the amount of data amassed. The system rests on the notion that if we have more information, we will be better positioned to make a decision. That is a false barometer for effectiveness, feeding the belief that through knowledge alone we know how to address our issues. Such a proclivity for data further thwarts the decision-making process and fuels an environment of indecision. In Friedman's opinion, this is actually a pathology that drives individuals on a futile quest for certainty, causing paralysis rather than progress.

Additionally, in such a system, empathy obviates responsibility. Related to a reliance on data, such an orientation toward feelings places the focus on weakness or immaturity rather than on strength.[20] The environment of an overly empathic system conspires against pastors to force acquiescence to the weakest or most immature individuals rather than holding those individuals accountable for their actions. When the motivation to confront challenges is lost (or becomes subverted by excessive and unhealthy empathy), the pastor's leadership is weakened while the congregation becomes ineffective.

How then do pastors master self-differentiation while avoiding the conforming issues that conspire to make leadership efforts ineffective? Author, psychologist, and science journalist Daniel Jay Goleman offers a strategy asserting that efficacy in leadership results from emotionally intelligent leaders who create resonance through skills such a motivating, guiding, inspiring, listening, and persuading.[21] Such leaders have the ability to create a synchronous connection with others to positively impact them from an emotional perspective. These emotionally intelligent leaders—those who are self-aware, self-managed, socially aware, and exhibit relationship management—are most efficacious.

Commonality with Friedman's theory is immediately evident in Goleman's idea of a pastoral leader who is self-aware. According to Goleman, self-aware leaders know themselves. They know their values and goals. They know what they stand for. They know where they are going and why. These are qualities also reflected in Bohn's research.

Reaching for self-knowledge and certainty is a life-long exercise. Warren G. Bennis, business theorist and leadership consultant, would suggest that self-knowledge requires us to recognize ourselves as our own best teacher, accept responsibility, given that we have the capacity to learn anything that we want to learn, and realize that true understanding comes from reflecting on our experiences.[22]

For Goleman, this is a critical point: "Self-aware people typically find time to reflect quietly."[23] This insight is at the heart of pastoral ministry. Through reflection, pastors can discern what is most important and gain a sense of a right or better way forward. This allows a pastor to act with conviction and certainty—a self-awareness that resonates and moves others to gladly follow.

Similar to Friedman's concept of a self-differentiated leader, Goleman's self-managed pastors have control of their emotions so they are not emotionally hijacked in times of stress or anxiety. These pastoral leaders are able to step back from self to gain a broader perspective on a situation. They are able to remain objective in order to achieve the church's goals. They can gauge the temperature of their congregation, modulate it, and help members make changes without being personally consumed by the emotions of the congregation. They remain positive and upbeat during times of stress and pressure so others can remain positively engaged.

Socially aware leaders, a third competency in Goleman's theory, demonstrate empathy and are able to grasp other people's feelings and perspectives.[24] For a pastoral leader, this means taking others' feelings and emotions into consideration in ways that build up and strengthen a congregation. At the same time, pastoral leaders who have this capacity for social awareness can draw on other emotional intelligence competencies so they do not fall prey to what Friedman would call an overly empathic system. These pastors are able to show compassion and empathy without being co-opted. Socially aware leaders also have the capacity to move us because they are in touch with our emotions, but they are not subject to them.

The final component of Goleman's emotional intelligence competencies is relationship management. Pastors who are adept at managing relationships demonstrate an authenticity that allows them to persuade, handle conflict, and increase collaborative efforts. Relationally managing leaders are able to inspire and excite people about their vision because they understand what people value and can articulate those values in a motivational way.

Considered together, Goleman's emotional intelligence competencies speak of self-differentiation. Abstracting his theory for the church, emotionally intelligent pastors know who they are—or more aptly, *whose* they are, and with such awareness, they discern the needs to address. Second, they can balance that know-how with an ability to consider others' feelings while managing relationships in a way that encourages people to get on board. It is self-differentiation that allows the pastor to lead in each of these dimensions. The result is efficacy in pastoral leadership.

Leaders with Know-How

Bohn's research indicates that leaders who instill certainty, clarity, and confidence realize efficacy in their leadership. This is certainly true for pastoral leaders as well. Congregants readily follow a pastor who exudes confidence and clarity in his or her call and purpose. However, Bohn also suggests that attributes such as credibility born from past accomplishments, clear communications, and task success positively impact efficacy as well. Consider the place for know-how. Credibility and task success speak to an analytical and conceptual capacity. Pastors must exhibit a level of knowledge that allows them to understand the specifics of a task or challenge. In many cases, this knowledge helps a pastor determine what needs to be done, which is a measure of efficacy. Ronald Heifetz would characterize such know-how as a technical capability. This means digestion of the necessary information has taken place to resolve the problem. Moreover, the solution has been put into a known set of procedures that guides the what, how, and who of the tasks at hand.[25]

The worship experience in our churches represents a technical capability. Worship is the most visible aspect of ministry in our churches. Therefore, pastors do well to exhibit a command of the order of worship and its implementation. Pastors have a responsibility to create coherence in worship, ensuring a connection between the liturgy, prayers, music, and sermon. Such coherence serves to enhance the congregational worship experience. Yet, this is a technical challenge we fully understand. Knowing our congregations, most pastors understand what to incorporate into the worship experience to create a positive effect.

At issue is the reality of many problems for which there are no technical solutions—because the know-how does not yet exist. Heifetz calls these types of problems adaptive challenges. For Heifetz, this is where a leader earns his or her stripes because leadership requires the leader to mobilize people to engage in the learning required to face, rather than avoid, the tough realities and conflicts encompassed in adaptive challenges.[26]

Consider the challenge of decline confronting many of our churches. There was a time when churches were full and bustling on a Sunday morning. In this environment, the greater challenges were internal—ensuring that there were enough Sunday school teachers that ministries were fully staffed, and that sufficient opportunities existed to satisfy the needs of a growing congregation. Today, as our congregations age and dwindle, churches need strategies for attracting people to their congregations.

These challenges are not resolved by simply changing our tried and true internal methods. These are challenges we do not know how to solve. It is what constitutes an adaptive challenge.

Mobilizing individuals to tackle such adaptive challenges is a core leadership strategy, as our environments become increasingly complex. Heifetz identifies a chief leadership tactic to create a holding environment: a psychoanalytic term whereby the stresses of the adaptive work are contained and regulated in a way that maintains enough tension to mobilize people, but not overwhelm.[27] This is a similar capability cited by Goleman in defining self-managed leaders. A self-managed pastoral leader must focus attention on ripening issues, not stress-reducing distractions. He or she does this by identifying and sharply focusing on issues that engage attention, while simultaneously counteracting efforts that lead to work avoidance. Efficacy is evident within this balance—when the pastor mobilizes people to meet a challenge, while maintaining an environment regulated by sufficient pressure.

Authentic and Level-5 Leaders

Other authors suggest additional means by which leadership efficacy is realized. For Bill George, efficacy is a result of being an authentic leader. An authentic leader is one who is self-aware, governed by established principles, intrinsically motivated, supported by a team, and demonstrates the existence of an integrated life.[28]

Similar to a self-differentiated or an emotionally intelligent leader, the authentic pastoral leader understands this quality of authenticity as part of his or her ministerial calling. These leaders are Spirit-led and motivated by the move of God in their lives. Their lives are a testimony that allows others to see pastoral leaders more clearly. Authenticity lived out this way is attractive and draws people to the authentic leader.

Additionally, an authentic leader must understand the values and principles that guide leadership. For pastoral leaders this includes recognizing and setting clear boundaries to determine the limits of acceptable action or behavior. Authentic leaders understand their intrinsic motivations. While George acknowledges the existence of externally recognized extrinsic motivations, such as monetary compensation, public recognition, and social status, he notes that intrinsic motivations, those derived from a personal sense of meaning in life, are the ones that create authenticity in leadership.[29] This assertion will certainly resonate with a pastoral leader.

Finally, an authentic leader requires relational structures for personal support. George suggests that authentic leaders have a support team who can be relied upon to undergird them along the way. This need is particularly true for pastors who are often plagued by loneliness in the pastoral vocation. Thus, collegial gatherings where pastors can work as a community of peers generate trusted relationships. Moreover, this time away from ministry to partake in such gatherings helps encourage pastors to establish balance within their personal and professional lives.

In fact, George emphasizes this point, indicating leaders must have personal strategies that allow them to remain grounded and integrated in life. Specifically, he suggests this self-awareness can only be achieved as the individual takes time for personal reflection or introspection.[30] It is a premise with which a pastoral leader can agree. Other strategies include finding time for one's self, maintaining spiritual practices to constantly clarify one's meaning and purpose in life, and maintaining relationships with friends and community. Considered in total, efficacy in pastoral leadership is realized when leaders hone their style and make authentic use of their power to generate superior performance from others with whom they are in contact.[31]

Jim Collins introduces a different term for the most efficacious leaders: Level 5 leaders. A Level 5 leader, according to Collins, is an individual who blends extreme personal humility with intense professional will.[32] This type of leader will have a number of traits that conspire to make him or her most effective.

First, Level 5 leaders demonstrate a paradoxical make up of humble modesty and willful fearlessness. Collins likens such individuals to Abraham Lincoln, suggesting Level 5 leaders never let ego get in the way of their primary ambition for the larger cause. Second, Level 5 leaders want to see their institution be even more successful in the next generation, despite recognizing that others may never attribute the roots of success to their efforts.[33] Level 5 leaders exhibit concern for the institution that exceeds concern for their own personal wealth or renown.

As pastoral leaders, these Level-5 characteristics are fitting. Paraphrasing the words of the apostle Paul, when we consider our calling, many of us were neither wise nor powerful. We were not noble by birth. Instead, we recognize God chose what is foolish in the world to shame the wise, what was weak to shame the strong, and what was low and despised in the world to reduce to nothing things that are, so that none would boast in the presence of God (1 Corinthians 1:26-29). Our strength as leaders comes through our humble submission to God. However, we also know we can do all things through Christ who strengthens us (Philippians 4:13). Thus, we are able to achieve that to which we are called.

Also in keeping with the Level 5 leader, pastors recognize that we have a responsibility to continue building up the body of Christ given the foundation, which is Jesus Christ. We are the builders who continue to build upon the foundation laid by those who came before us. Thus, pastoral leaders aspire to embody the characteristics of Level 5 leaders, acknowledging our calling with modest humility and going about our work in self-effacing ways. Nevertheless, we are equally ferocious in our resolve to do whatever is necessary to make the church great.

Interestingly, Collins notes it is this combination of traits—humility and determination—that distinguishes Level 5 leaders from servant leaders. Most pastors are familiar with servant leadership, a model whereby those being served become healthier, wiser, more autonomous, and more likely to become servants to others.[34] Moreover, servant leaders are most concerned with taking care of the needs of other people first. I contend that most pastors are servant leaders. While Collins would recognize such traits as admirable, he and his team would argue that it is necessary to see "both sides of the coin."[35] Level 5 leaders are humble and also driven by an unwavering resolve.

Finally, Level 5 leaders are ones who will apportion credit to factors outside of themselves when things go well, while apportioning responsibility when things go poorly.[36] Pastors who are Level 5 leaders will not take the credit for their congregation's success. Rather, they emphasize the role of others. In like fashion, given problems or challenges, Level 5 leaders "look in the mirror" to reflect and appropriately identify responsibility for resolving the problem.

In fact, this point stands out in becoming a Level 5 leader. Collins quickly noted that while the scope of his research did not yield a list of steps for becoming a Level 5 leader, self-reflection did stand out as chief among the possible factors that may contribute to the development of Level 5 leaders.

You Can Learn, Too

What have we learned thus far? That leadership and efficacy are correlated; that the behavioral qualities contributing to efficacy in leadership include the ability to convey or communicate certainty, focus, and credibility; and that these behavioral qualities can be seen in self-differentiated, emotionally intelligent, adaptively capable, authentic, Level 5 leaders.

Wow, what an incredibly tall order! Is it possible for a pastoral leader to do all of this? Yes, according to Goleman, whose research demonstrates that the competencies which lead to efficacy are not innate talents, but learned abilities. This assertion is supported by Robert Kegan and Lisa Laskow Lahey, scholars who have developed a process to demonstrate and document the capacity to realize such learning. Their book, *Immunity to Change*, demonstrates that anyone can achieve higher levels of mental capacity, thereby increasing effectiveness, flexibility, and the capacity to respond adaptively to the challenges that life presents.

The concept of increased mental capacity is an extension of Kegan's evolutionary truce theory, the process by which the individual moves from being subject to their perspectives to being individuated from them.[37] As we increase our mental capacity, we are able to objectify and be less subjected to our personal thoughts and feelings, enabling us to meet the complexity of the world's demands with greater adaptability.[38]

This research is significant given the realization that mental capacity does not plateau in early adulthood, but rather tends to increase with age.[39] Furthermore, as complexity increases, research shows there are three discernibly distinct plateaus, each providing an epistemological means by which an adult makes sense of the world. The socialized mind is shaped and therefore held by the definitions and expectations of the individual's personal environment. In contrast, the *self-authoring mind* objectively steps back from the socialized expectations, but remains subject to one's personal filter and bias. The *self-transforming mind* objectifies its own personal filter, thus providing space to fully consider all possible options.

Each plateau outperforms the mental complexity of the lower level. Thus, our ability to respond adaptively to challenges increases significantly as we advance to more sophisticated stages of mental development.[40] The underlying premise is that as we advance in our adaptive responsiveness, we become more effective. More specifically, Kegan and Lahey suggest our continued maturity makes it possible for us to realize greater objectivity in decision making. What we must overcome during this maturation process is what they call *cultural embeddedness*, which is a bias based on personal upbringing and socialization that leads us to project our subjectivity onto the world in our constitution of reality.[41] In short, this embeddedness becomes a limiting factor and an obstacle in realizing mental maturity. It is not necessarily a negative factor, however. Embeddedness also serves as a highly effective, anxiety-management, immune system.[42] That immune system keeps individuals in balance. Therefore, it becomes necessary to build a more expansive immune system, which serves to overcome the limiting factors of our embedded bias while maintaining balance.

Mental balance happens when we identify assumptions that sustain our immune system. As long as these assumptions hold, we remain at our current stage of mental development, meaning that we are subject to the behaviors that thwart our ability to change. However, as we are able to test and disprove our assumptions, we experience release from the constraints of our current immunity to change, because we emerge from our embeddedness. As we gain mental complexity, we realize greater efficacy.

A colleague shared how she consistently overextended herself in her consulting practice. When she stopped to assess the reason for that, she realized it was because she said yes to every engagement request she received. She would tell herself she needed to be more discerning about the requests and not accept every one, but regardless of her mental pep talks, the results would be the same. She invariably said yes in response to all requests.

This colleague recognized the need to step back and assess the situation. She realized that what was going on was an underlying fear, namely that by saying no to an engagement, she would alienate the requester and no longer be liked. This became a foundational assumption. As long as that fear was in place, she could not say no to a request. She was embedded in and subject to her fear.

Not until she challenged her assumption was she able to make a change in her life. As an experiment, she decided to say no to an engagement if she did not feel really drawn toward it. Then, she would test the results of having said no to determine whether or not ill-will resulted on the part of the requestor. What she learned was that people did not dislike her for saying no. By testing her assumption, she found it was not always true—and she discovered an expanded perspective.

The means by which to expand mental capacity is reflection. In the words of professors and authors Chris Argyris and Donald Schön, "All human beings need to become competent in taking action and simultaneously reflecting on this action to learn from it."[43] This is a significant finding, particularly when considering pastoral leadership. Reflection is not only one of the sustaining practices for ministry, but it is recommended by experts as a chief practice for all leaders.

More specifically in their research, Argyris and Schön introduce the notion of theories-in-use. A theory is a set of interconnected propositions that are recursively traversed to achieve some desired action. Thus a theory-in-use is the theory that actually governs an individual's actions as observed by the individual's behavior.[44] According to the authors, a theory-in-use is effective when an implemented theory tends to achieve its governing variables.[45] In other words, if the theories we use achieve our desired goals without violating a held belief or principle, the theory-in-use is effective. However, we must test our theories to determine if the desired actions have been achieved.

In the long run, effectiveness is dependent on the ability to learn new ways of managing the dynamics of a changing environment. Strategies are required to help individuals not only to achieve efficacy in their actions, but to also maintain efficacy in the long run. To accomplish this, the authors' studies demonstrate that individuals must be able to look forward in order to predict the consequences of their behavior, look backward in order to examine the governing variables of the behavior, and then identify the feedback that impedes change.[46] Through such reflection individuals are able to obtain knowledge about their actions and make the necessary corrections to expansively move forward. It is a process of efficacy in action, made possible by reflection.

What Have We Learned?

We have learned that a chief focus of leadership is efficacy. Maximizing the generative capacity of a congregation or an organization while balancing the demands and challenges of the opportunities it encounters—the measure of efficacy—is the responsibility of leadership. Given this responsibility and its correlation to how leadership positively impacts efficacy, several leadership theorists and authors have identified self-differentiation, emotional intelligence, and adaptive, authentic, Level-5 leadership as means by which a pastoral leader can realize efficacy.

Trying to possess all of these qualities may seem like an elusive endeavor, but the good news is there is hope. We can learn how to be such leaders as we increase our mental capacity and operate more adaptively in our environment. As we expand our mental model, we emerge from cultural embeddedness to objectivity. This enables us to view and assess the world in more differentiated ways. This expansion is sustainable through the practice of reflection.

Reflection was cited as key to achieving efficacy in leadership by multiple leadership theorists. For Friedman, self-differentiation is attained through an inner, reflective focus. Both Goleman and George explicitly note self-aware people take time to reflect. Collins also identified reflection as one of the possible factors for becoming a Level 5 leader.

Thus, reflection—the opportunity to create time and space to think clearly about one's life or to consider actions performed in order to determine how those actions need to change to realize greater success—serves as the common catalyst. It, therefore, seems appropriate to conclude that the ability to reflect and determine appropriate action based on such reflection is what leads to true efficacy in pastoral leadership. By the same token, it stands to reason that the ability to be reflective requires a leader to take time apart in order to practice such reflection.

How do we do that? This question will be the focus of Chapter 2.

NOTES

1. Ronald A. Heifetz defines leadership as "engaging people to make progress on the adaptive problems that they face," in *Leadership without Easy Answers* (Cambridge, MA: The Belknap Press of Harvard University Press, 1994), 187. He defines adaptive leadership as "the practice of mobilizing people to tackle tough challenges and thrive," in *The Practice of Adaptive Leadership: Tools and Tactics for Changing Your Organization and the World* (Boston: Harvard Business Review Press, 2009), 14. Heifetz incorporates the notion of learning in adaptive work noting that "Adaptive work consists of the learning required to address conflicts in the values people hold, or to diminish the gap between the values people stand for and the reality they face," (Heifetz, *Leadership*, 22). These concepts of mobilizing others to learn in order to face organizational challenges are brought together in this definition.

2. James G. Bohn, "The Design and Development of an Instrument to Measure Organizational Efficacy," Proceedings of the Academy of Human Resources Development 2002 Conference, Volume 2: Symposium 21: Organization Development, 540; Honolulu, Hawaii, February 27–March 3, 2002.

3. Daniel Goleman, Richard Boyatzis, and Annie McKee, *Primal Leadership: Learning to Lead with Emotional Intelligence* (Boston: Harvard Business School Press, 2004), 3.

4. James M. Kouzes and Barry Z. Posner, *The Leadership Challenge* (San Francisco: Jossey-Bass Publishers, 1987), xv.

5. Eugene H. Peterson, *THE MESSAGE: The Bible in Contemporary Language* (Colorado Springs: NavPress, 2002), 1155.

6. Max De Pree, *Leadership Is an Art* (New York: Currency Doubleday, 2004), 19.

7. De Pree, 19.

8. Bill George, *True North: Discover Your Authentic Leadership* (San Francisco: Jossey-Bass, 2007), 185.

9. Jim Collins, *Good to Great: Why Some Companies Make the Leap . . . and Others Don't* (New York: HarperCollins, 2001), 20.

10. Collins, 205.

11. James G. Bohn, "The Relationship of Perceived Leadership Behaviors to Organizational Efficacy," *Journal of Leadership and Organizational Studies*, Volume 9, No. 2, 2002, 66.

12. Bohn, 76.

13. Edwin H. Friedman, *A Failure of Nerve: Leadership in the Age of the Quick Fix* (New York: Seabury Books, 2007), 191.

14. Friedman, 14.

15. Friedman, 203.

16. George, 71.

17. George, 53.

18. Robert E. Quinn, *Deep Change: Discovering the Leader Within* (San Francisco: Jossey-Bass, 1996), 136.

19. Friedman, 69.

20. Friedman, 134.

21. Goleman, Boyatzis, and McKee, 27.

22. Warren G. Bennis, *On Becoming a Leader* (Reading, MA: Addison-Wesley Publishing Company), 56.

23. Goleman, Boyatis, and McKee, 40.

24. Goleman, Boyatis, and McKee, 50.

25. Heifetz, *Leadership*, 71–72.

26. Heifetz, *Leadership*, 22.
27. Heifetz, *Leadership*, 105–106.
28. George, 66.
29. George, 106–107.
30. George, 78.
31. George, 151.
32. Collins, 21.
33. Collins, 26.
34. Robert K. Greenleaf, *The Servant as Leader* (Indianapolis: Robert K. Greenleaf Center, 1991), 7.
35. Collins, 30.
36. Collins, 35.
37. Robert Kegan, *The Evolving Self: Problem and Process in Human Development* (Cambridge, MA: Harvard University Press, 1982), 29.
38. Robert Kegan and Lisa Laskow Lahey, *Immunity to Change: How to Overcome it and Unlock the Potential in Yourself and Your Organization* (Boston: Harvard Business Press, 2009), 30.
39. Kegan and Lahey, 14.
40. Kegan and Lahey, 29.
41. Kegan, 31.
42. Kegan and Lahey, 41.
43. Chris Argyris and Donald A. Schön, *Theory in Practice: Increasing Professional Effectiveness* (San Francisco: Jossey-Bass, 1974), 4.
44. Argyris and Schön, 7.
45. Argyris and Schön, 24.
46. Argyris and Schön, 99.

·2·

time apart

AS CHAPTER 1 demonstrated, pastoral leaders who engage in reflection are more effective in their leadership. Of course, the challenge is to take time apart from leadership to engage in reflection. Too often, this is easier said than done because the demands of pastoral leadership make it difficult to take time apart. Yet, if we would make such reflective space away from leadership, we would recognize that not only is time apart a beneficial strategy, it is also a critical requirement for leadership.

To make this point, we will consider time apart from three different perspectives. First, we will explore the practice that leadership expert Ronald Heifetz calls sanctuary. Sanctuary provides the necessary physical or mental space for renewal. Second, we will recognize sabbath as God-ordained time apart. Through sabbath, humanity is refreshed and renewed. Finally, we will consider the time-apart practices of Jesus—Jesus observed Sabbath within Jewish religious tradition, but he also engaged in a daily sabbath practice during which he took time apart for renewal and restoration in the midst of ministry. Each of these three perspectives commends taking time apart. Reflection becomes possible when we take time apart to refresh.

The Practice of Finding Sanctuary

Author and academic Ronald Heifetz consistently recommends to leaders the practice of finding sanctuary. What is sanctuary? Sanctuaries are those physical or mental spaces in which people can be present to their inner voice and the quieter inclinations of their spirit.[1] As pastoral leaders, it is critical that we create this kind of space in the midst of ministry. At times when pastoral leaders are consumed in the numerous demands and challenges of their work, they need a space where they can renew their sense of purpose and reaffirm their sense of call.

Sanctuary becomes the place to distance oneself from the challenges in order to objectively consider options and regain perspective. This space also makes it possible for leaders to feel certain about the decisions they make because sanctuary provides that opportunity to step back and reassess.

Sanctuary is also critical for adaptive leadership. Many of the issues pastoral leaders face are beyond the basic technical challenges of ministry. In addition to preaching and teaching, pastoral leaders are executives, administrators, community builders, counselors, and more. To be successful given the variety of roles, leaders must also acknowledge we do not have the answers. Instead, we benefit from bringing together diverse voices to collaborate and learn in order to make progress. Part of our role as leaders is modeling how to rely on others and creating an environment that makes engagement and interaction possible.

This way of leading requires objectivity, a healthy distance that permits a broader perspective. Sanctuary becomes the place that offers such distance while supplying the courage needed to sustain us as we adaptively lead. Just as leadership demands a strategy of mobilizing people, it also requires a strategy of deploying and restoring one's own spiritual resources.[2] Sanctuary is the place and space.

Time Apart as Sabbath

Time apart is a practice reflected in the Jewish faith tradition, specifically as considered through the lens of Sabbath, which honors the seventh day of the week as a day of rest. Rabbi and scholar

Abraham Joshua Heschel likens Sabbath to a sanctuary in time. Because one day is set apart for rest and worship, time becomes the vehicle through which people connect to God. As Heschel notes time is the presence of God in the world of space, and it is within time that we are able to sense the unity of all beings.[3] This is the notion and plan of Sabbath. God gave Sabbath to humanity for our physical and spiritual renewal. It is the recognition that for six days a week, our time is spent making, shaping, and transforming the world. Human beings function as creators, just as God created. However, on this one day apart, we change our relationship to the world—by refraining from acting upon the world and instead standing back and celebrating the grandeur and mystery of creation.[4]

This definition and vaulted view of Sabbath is observed in the Creation narrative recorded in Genesis 2:2-3: "And on the seventh day God finished the work that he had done, and he rested on the seventh day from all the work that he had done. So God blessed the seventh day and hallowed it, because on it God rested from all the work that he had done in creation."

In this narrative, we recognize that God finished the work of Creation and rested on the seventh day. This act of resting, called Sabbath, is derived from the Hebrew verb *shâbath*, a primitive root that means to repose, or to desist from exertion.[5] The meaning of this translation denotes cessation of work rather than relaxation or rest. God created and, being satisfied with creation, God stopped. Citing author Dorothy Bass, Tony Jones notes that in the ceasing,

> God declares as fully as possible just how very good creation is. In resting, God takes pleasure in what has been made; God has no regrets, no need to go on to create a still better world or creature more wonderful than the man and woman. In the day of rest, God's free love toward humanity takes form as time shared with them.[6]

Sabbath is set apart not only by virtue of the fact that God ceased work, but also because God blessed the seventh day. This blessing is significant because the seventh day is the only day God blesses. Prior to blessing the seventh day, God blesses the creatures of the sea and birds (Genesis 1:22) and humanity (Genesis 1:28). At its most literal level, the Hebrew root *barak*, to bless, describes the bending of the knee which is an act of humility associated with worship and praise.[7] More generally, to bless means to extend greetings or well wishes. However, God's blessings connote a greater meaning. God's blessings are recognized not simply as "good wishes," but as the assurance of fruitfulness, prosperity, and a happy and abundant life.[8] God blessed creatures and humanity as a means of ensuring prosperity and abundance. Yet, through the blessing of time, Sabbath becomes God's desire for humanity. Sabbath is a means to assure fruitfulness, prosperity, and the like. In return, by observing the blessed Sabbath, humanity takes time apart, and through worship, we express our gratefulness to God.

Moreover, God set time apart by desisting activity, thereby designating that time as holy. Nothing else in creation is endowed with such a quality of holiness.[9] Time was hallowed by God and sanctified because it was set apart. Because God set Sabbath apart, we are to remember the Sabbath as and regard it as holy.

This holy use of time is commended to humanity in Exodus 16. In the wilderness, God provided manna. The Israelites were instructed to collect only what was needed per person on a daily basis. However, on the sixth day they were instructed to gather twice as much manna as was needed so that on the seventh day they might honor God's commandment for a holy Sabbath as a solemn day of rest (Exodus 16:23, 26). From this narrative, Sabbath is initially instituted as a day free of any forays in gathering manna, to be held instead as a day of waiting for God's fulfillment of his word.[10]

Additional prohibitions were enjoined to Sabbath observance as noted in the Decalogue. Deuteronomy 5:12-15 instructs:

> Observe the Sabbath day and keep it holy, as the LORD your God commanded you. Six days you shall labor and do all your work. But the seventh day is a Sabbath to the LORD your God; you shall not do any work—you, or your son or your daughter, or your male or female slave, or your ox or your donkey, or any of your livestock, or the resident alien in your towns, so that your male and female slave may rest as well as you. Remember that you were a slave in the land of Egypt, and the LORD your God brought you out from there with a mighty hand and an outstretched arm; therefore the LORD your God commanded you to keep the Sabbath day.

The Sabbath was to be a day of ceasing work for all who resided in Israel, including servants, resident aliens, and their livestock. Having been required to work seven days a week under the bondage of slavery in Egypt, God reminded Israel of the importance of keeping Sabbath. Moreover, the command for a weekly observance was made explicit. With the Sabbath, the commandment to rest exactly after six days of work as God did is mandated, and in doing so, humanity functions in God's image and likeness.[11]

Sabbath observance is expressed fully in Exodus 31. Moving beyond a prohibition of gathering food and the association with Creation, Exodus 31:15 mandates a day of complete rest from all types of work. Sabbath comes to represent a perpetual covenant between God and Israel. In fact, Sabbath observance is so important that those who violate it are put to death. Sabbath is one of Israel's most sacred times, created with a redemptive and celebratory quality that served to protect and promote the elements of provision, creation, and covenant.[12]

Thus, if it is commended that individuals find sanctuary in order to restore their sense of purpose, put issues in perspective, and regain courage and heart, and if such restoration can be achieved through the observance of Sabbath, which commands us to cease work to rest, worship, and receive the blessings of God—then we can conclude that sanctuary can be found through honoring Sabbath.

However, the Christian faith tradition has not observed the Sabbath in this same manner as held by the Jews. This may have been as a result of second-century Christian teaching maintaining that Christ liberated us from the law such that the command to observe the Sabbath was eliminated.[13] This belief seems to be supported when we consider Jesus' relationship with the Sabbath.

Jesus and Observing Sabbath

The Synoptic Gospels cite various occasions when Jesus' actions suggested a failure to refrain from ceasing work on the Sabbath. In one instance, Jesus is challenged by the Pharisees because his disciples are found gleaning wheat to satisfy their hunger on the Sabbath (Matthew 12:1-8; Mark 2:23-28; Luke 6:1-5). The Gospels also recount several instances when Jesus healed on the Sabbath.[14]

Given that these actions would be considered as engaging in work, how are we to interpret them?

While the Sabbath was set aside as a holy day to remember God's act of Creation and sanctified for humanity's spiritual renewal, its observance had changed by Jesus' time. The Sabbath had become legalized with specific requirements and demands imposed upon it to such an extent that Sabbath had lost its original meaning and had become a burden rather than a delight.[15] There was greater concern in observing the letter of the law rather than attending to the needs of humanity. In light of this narrowed, legalistic interpretation of Sabbath, Jesus responded.

Against the charge of gleaning wheat on the Sabbath, Jesus reminded the Pharisees of David's actions when he and his companions were hungry and in need of food (see 1 Samuel 21:1-6). David entered the house of God and not only ate the bread of the Presence, which was reserved for the priests, but also gave some to his companions. Having reminded the Pharisee of this history, Jesus continued his teachings. Specifically, Jesus asserted that the Sabbath was made for humankind and not humankind for the Sabbath. Jesus' argument was rooted in the fact that humanity was made first, and the Sabbath was appointed for humanity's welfare, such that the law respecting it must not be interpreted so as to oppose humanity's real welfare.[16]

In other words, the Sabbath is subservient to the needs of those for whom it was created. As Hebrew essayist and leading Zionist thinker Ahad Ha'am remarked, "More than Jews have kept the Sabbath, Sabbath has kept the Jews."[17] His remark reflected the conviction that, because of the regulation of time commanded by Sabbath, the opportunity to come together as community has been the foundation that has sustained Jewish identity.

It was this concern for community to which Jesus spoke. The Jews maintained it was lawful to save life on the Sabbath, but not to heal an illness or tend to an injury. From the perspective of the Pharisees, a non-life threatening situation did not require action; thus, healing on the Sabbath was unlawful. Yet, for Jesus, human need was of utmost importance, and the Sabbath was not intended to be a hindrance in the performance of deeds of mercy.[18]

Jesus' healings restored people so they could fully thrive and enjoy the delights of Sabbath. This is an important point because none of the people Jesus healed on the Sabbath were ritualistically estranged or prohibited from participating in a Sabbath observance. But Jesus' healing was an act of mercy and represented God's desire for humanity: a renewed, restored relationship with an infinitely merciful God.

It also must be observed that Jesus did attend to some traditions of the Sabbath. As Luke 4:16 notes, "When [Jesus] came to Nazareth, where he had been brought up, he went to the synagogue on the Sabbath day, as was his custom." Similar examples are cited in Mark 1:21; 3:1; and Luke 13:10. Jesus regularly attended the synagogue on the Sabbath day. From this it is clear Jesus' customary practice was to observe the Sabbath by attending the synagogue— by sanctifying time for the purpose of connecting with God in worship with the community of faith.

Thus, Jesus kept the Sabbath as one who was faithful to the law. Yet, he challenged the petty enforcements of its subsidiary rules and regulations, which were developed by the Pharisees.[19] Since Sabbath was made and given for humanity, Jesus' actions effectively restored God's intent for Sabbath.

Moreover, Jesus elevated the notion of taking time apart to extend beyond the seventh day Sabbath observation. Jesus did not wait for the Sabbath to observe time apart. He demonstrated the idea of a daily sabbath, where time apart was intentionally sought and regularly observed during the course of the day and night. In Mark 1, on the day following the Sabbath, Jesus retreated very early in the morning while it was still dark to a deserted place where he prayed (Mark 1:35). The parallel Scripture in Luke 4:42 omits reference to prayer as a motivation for time apart and notes Jesus' departure at daybreak, thereby suggesting the reason for Jesus' solitude was simply to get away from the crowds.[20] While his reasoning for departure in these two passages is inconclusive, it is clear Jesus began his day seeking time apart prior to engaging in ministry.

In Mark 6:46, Jesus left the crowds after feeding them, late at night, seeking time apart for prayer in the mountains. Jesus also sought time apart to pray in the mountains at night as suggested by Luke 6:12. Jesus did not explain his reasons for seeking time apart, instead of closing out the day in corporate prayer with his disciples. But his example of disengaging from ministry at the end of the day stands as a model for his followers. Jesus created space to intentionally seek God—a sabbath practice not delimited by a day of the week.

In this practice, Jesus demonstrated that taking time apart at any time was an effective means of self-care in the midst of a growing ministry. As Jesus' fame spread, the numbers of people who came to hear and be healed by him increased. Untold numbers of individuals were brought to Jesus with sickness and a variety of diseases. The Scriptures suggest that such ministry demands were depleting.

In Luke 6:17, as a result of the crowds attempting to touch Jesus, virtue (or power) went out of his body, yet he healed them all. A similar occurrence is documented in Luke 8:45, where Jesus physically sensed virtue leaving his body when the woman who suffered from hemorrhages touched him. In response, Jesus withdrew to deserted places to pray (Luke 5:15-16; John 6:15). This practice of retreating became a means for Jesus to be sustained and refreshed in the midst of ministry.

Perhaps this is nowhere more evident than in Mark 4:35-41. In the preceding narrative, Jesus had begun to teach by the sea. Such a large crowd had gathered to hear Jesus that he was forced into a boat from which he taught, presumably for the entire day. Verse 35 relates that, when evening arrived, Jesus told his disciples to cross to the other side of the sea. He promptly retreated to the stern of the boat and fell sound asleep on a cushion. As pastor and author Kirk Byron Jones notes, "Jesus' perfection did not exempt him from taking care of the human body that he occupied."[21] Having ministered through the entire day, Jesus was tired and required sleep in what Jones termed "the back of the boat." Jones likened this "back of the boat time" to sabbath, a mandated time through which Jesus could realize a healthy, balanced, and productive life.[22]

Jesus also sought time apart during times of distress and difficulty. In the garden of Gethsemane, Jesus engaged in what was for him a regular habit; he took time apart as someone who always found strength in prayer. He was praying as someone seeking strength for the present moment, rather than crying out despairingly as someone unfamiliar with the practice.[23] Similarly, in Jesus' final words on the cross, he quoted the first line of Psalm 22 and with his last breath prayed, "Father, into your hands I commit my spirit!"(Luke 23:46). Although Jesus hung on the cross, having been made a public display, he used prayer to take time apart with God in his last moments.

Jesus also used time apart through prayer prior to making decisions or during great moments in ministry. When he was baptized, Jesus was also praying (Luke 3:21). Before choosing the twelve disciples, Jesus went out to a mountain and prayed all night to God (Luke 6:12-13). Jesus was prayerful in the moments before he asked the disciples, "Who do you say I am?" (Luke 9:18), and he was in prayer in those moments when the disciples saw him transfigured (9:28). Mark 6 records two of Jesus' most notable miracles—the feeding of the 5,000 and the walking on water—and in both cases, Scripture records that Jesus was in prayer just before the miracles (see vv. 30-32; vv. 45-46). These examples cause author James D. G. Dunn to conclude that prayer was most likely Jesus' regular response during times of crisis or decision.[24]

Thus, Jesus took time apart to be sustained and restored in the ministry, but he also modeled these acts of time apart for his disciples. Luke 9:18 and 11:1 suggest Jesus took time apart to pray while only the disciples were near him. In doing this, Jesus effectively commended these practices to his disciples so they might also recognize the benefit of time apart and engage in these practices for themselves. They were able to see this rhythm of ministry and retreat and to recognize firsthand the power that came from such engagement. In fact, this pattern was so effective that one of the disciples was moved to ask, "Lord, teach us to pray as John taught his disciples" (Luke 11:1).

Nevertheless, just as the disciples of Jesus' day struggled to learn the practice of engaging and retreating, as modern-day disciples we also continue to struggle with the notion of sabbath and taking time apart. Kirk Jones concurs, indicating that our time spent in the "back of the boat" makes the "on" time possible, yet there are formidable obstructions to getting to the back of the boat.[25]

First, we delude ourselves with a personal sense of indispensability. This is particularly true for those engaged in the work of ministry. It is as though ministers have taken to heart the words of Charles Haddon Spurgeon, a Baptist preacher, who said, "A minister, whatever he [sic] is, is a minister and should recollect that he is on duty; a policeman or a soldier may be off duty, but a minister never is."[26] However, this is a dangerous belief. To accept

Spurgeon's definition of commitment is to accept uncritically the myth of human indispensability.

Author Wayne Muller also suggests that human beings are often afraid to rest. If we rest, we might stop and listen, finding a lurking emptiness, a terrible, aching void with nothing to fill it, as if it will corrode and destroy us like some horrible, insatiable monster.[27] As a result, the human tendency is to fill every possible space with tasks, errands, and things to do to avoid this emptiness. While this may be a valid assertion for some, Muller's assumption is as potentially dangerous as Spurgeon's. Many would argue against the notion that failure to stop is motivated by a personal fear of rest. At times failure to stop is more of the reality of life.

Yet, we have Jesus' example to demonstrate the value of time apart. Even as the disciples hunted for Jesus (Mark 1:36-37), Jesus honored a deep spiritual need for a time dedicated not to accomplishment and growth, but to quiescence and rest.[28] These are the two phases of dormancy, Muller argues, and both quiescence and rest are required for a seed to maximize its strength and fruitfulness.

We are no different. We, too, need a period of quietness and inactivity when we are not ruffled by passions or quickened by events. It is in this down time and rest that we can be restored. We need to learn to take time apart, recognizing that in doing so, we are strengthened and made fruitful.

This notion is reminiscent of Exodus 31. According to the Talmudic commentator Rashi, God appreciated the difficulty in keeping Sabbath. Rashi translates Exodus 31:13 saying, "Verily my Sabbaths you shall keep even though you will be anxious and eager in (your) zeal for work."[29] But, it was critical for Israel to maintain God's command, not only because of the mandate, but also because of the result. As God rested on the seventh day, God was refreshed. "The Hebrew word used for refreshed, *va-yinnafash*, is derived from the noun *nefesh*, a term that can refer to a person's life essence, vitality, psychic energy or essential character."[30] By ceasing work and resting, God experienced an infusion of spiritual and physical vigor to the extent that it served to revive God's entire being. In short, through rest, God received a new soul.

This same kind of refreshment and restoration is commended to humanity. As humanity ceases work in order to observe time as holy unto God, humanity is refreshed. The original commandment came in the form of a seventh-day Sabbath. However, in the ministry of Jesus, we recognize his engagement with times of ceasing and rest was not limited only to the Sabbath day, but daily sabbaths were a regular spiritual practice. Moreover, we recognize that as Jesus engaged in time apart, praying, and communing with God, he experienced restoration and he was refreshed for the continuing work of ministry.

What Have We Learned?

As we see in this chapter, whether observed in weekly Sabbath or in a regular rhythm of daily sabbath practices, time apart is beneficial. It was commended by God and practiced by Jesus. Time apart provides refreshment, restoration, blessings, and fruitfulness. It is the consecration of time that allows us to quiet ourselves to receive God's blessings. It is the reminder to stop, to cease work and refrain from even thinking about our tasks.

Moreover, if as followers of Jesus we observe his ministry, we can recognize the need for daily sabbath; that is, time apart in order to be restored in the midst of our ministry and work. From Jesus' example, we note that time apart provides relief from stress, prepares us for decision making, and provides refreshment during times of depletion. In short, the result of this time apart can be seen in Heifetz's definition of sanctuary: it becomes the means by which individuals restore their spiritual resources.

Considered from these perspectives, creating sanctuary is not simply an optional activity. It becomes a critical requirement for leadership because it allows the leader to be restored and refreshed, thereby creating the capacity to be effective in leadership.

Yet, this realization begs the question: Is there something particular we should do during our time apart? The Torah provides the basic rules for what is and is not acceptable on the Sabbath. However, a dense and complex oral law was created over the centuries as rabbis posed and answered questions and case studies.[31] Jesus' observances of time apart were void of specific prohibitions. Nevertheless, in each of the Synoptic Gospel references, Jesus sought time apart for prayer, but is this the sole task for spiritual engagement during time apart?

Heifetz commends time apart, but he carefully avoids dictating particular practices for this time. He says quite adamantly, "We're not peddling a particular type of sanctuary."[32] For Heifetz, what is done to create sanctuary is a personal choice and can vary widely depending on the individual. Rather than mandating a particular sanctuary, Heifetz commends finding sanctuary that fits the individual as a structure to promote reflection and protect daily engagement.[33]

Nevertheless, leadership experts seem to commend a synthesis of weekly and daily sabbath keeping. Through sabbath, we recognize the benefits of refreshment and blessings. Moreover, as we protect the time of sabbath for daily engagement, we can realize strength and renewal in the moment. Certainly, such engagement increases our capacity to be effective as leaders, because we are more effective when refreshed.

I would further contend that what we do during our time apart also matters. In taking time apart, it stands to reason certain practices will promote greater reflection. Such practices would help us to project forward and backward in order to determine the actions that impede change. Said another way, we want to engage in efforts to help us reflect on our image of the ideal in order to align ourselves to that ideal. This type of engagement is the practice of spirituality, and spirituality is the focus of Chapter 3.

NOTES

1. Ronald A. Heifetz, Alexander Grashow, and Marty Linsky, *The Practice of Adaptive Leadership: Tools and Tactics for Changing Your Organization and the World* (Boston: Harvard Business Press, 2009), 294.

2. Ronald A. Heifetz, *Leadership without Easy Answers* (Boston: Harvard University Press, 1998), 273–274.

3. Abraham Joshua Heschel, *The Sabbath* (New York: Farrar, Straus and Giroux, 1979), 100.

4. Marva J. Dawn, *Keeping the Sabbath Wholly: Ceasing, Resting, Embracing, Feasting* (Grand Rapids, MI: Eerdmans Publishing Company, 1989), 204.

5. James Strong, *Strong's Hebrew and Greek Dictionaries—Electronic STEP Files Edition* (Cedar Rapids, IA: Parsons Technology, Inc., 1998).

6. Tony Jones, *The Sacred Way: Spiritual Practices for Everyday Life* (El Cajon, CA: Youth Specialties, 2005), 180.

7. Richard H. Lowery, *Sabbath and Jubilee* (St. Louis, MO: Chalice Press, 2000), 90.

8. Samuele Bacchiocchi, "The Sabbath in Jewish and Christian Traditions," *Remembering the Sabbath: The Creation-Sabbath in Jewish and Christian History*, eds.

Tamara Cohn Eskenazi, Daniel J. Harrington, and William H. Shea (New York: The Crossroad Publishing Company, 1991), 75.

9. Heschel, 9.

10. Daniel C. Timmer, *Creation, Tabernacle, and Sabbath: The Sabbath Frame of Exodus 31:12-17; 35:1-3 in Exegetical and Theological Perspective* (Germany: Vanderhoeck & Ruprecht, 2009), 47.

11. Christopher D. Ringwald, *A Day Apart: How Jews, Christians, and Muslims Find Faith, Freedom, and Joy on the Sabbath* (New York: Oxford University Press, 2007), 18.

12. Timmer, 51.

13. Ringwald, 85.

14. Matthew 12:9-14, Mark 3:2-6, and Luke 6:6-11 recount the narrative of Jesus healing the man with the withered hand; Luke 13:10-16 recounts the narrative of Jesus healing the woman with a spirit that had crippled her for 18 years; Luke 14:1-6 recounts the narrative of Jesus healing the man with dropsy; John 5:1-18 recounts the narrative of Jesus healing the man who had been ill for 38 years; and John 9:14-34 recounts the narrative of Jesus restoring sight to a man who was blind from birth.

15. Herbert E. Saunders, *The Sabbath: Symbol of Creation and Re-Creation* (Plainfield, NJ: American Sabbath Tract Society, 1970), 34.

16. Albert Barnes, *Barnes' Notes on the New Testament—Electronic Edition* (Cedar Rapids, IA: 1999), Mark 2:27.

17. Judith Shulevitz, "How the Sabbath keeps the Jewish people." Accessed January 26, 2012. http://www.haaretz.com/jewish-world/2.209/how-the-sabbath-keeps-the-jewish-people-1.283841.

18. Saunders, 43.

19. Henry Sturcke, *Encountering the Rest of God: How Jesus Came to Personify the Sabbath* (Zurich: Theologischer Verlag Zurich, 2005), 70.

20. I. Howard Marshall, "Jesus—Example and Teacher of Prayer in the Synoptic Gospels," *Into God's Presence: Prayer in the New Testament*, ed. Richard N. Longenecker (Grand Rapids, MI: William B. Eerdmans Publishing Company, 2001), 117.

21. Kirk Byron Jones, *Rest in the Storm: Self-Care Strategies for Clergy and Other Caregivers* (Valley Forge, PA: Judson Press, 2001), 25.

22. Kirk Byron Jones, 26, 42

23. James D. G. Dunn, *Jesus and the Spirit: A Study of the Religious and Charismatic Experience of Jesus and the First Christians as Reflected in the New Testament* (Grand Rapids, MI: William B. Eerdmans Publishing Company, 1997), 20.

24. Dunn, 21.

25. KB Jones, 27.

26. G. Golden Pike, *Sermons of Rev. C. H. Spurgeon* (New York: Funk & Wagnalls Company, 1892), 158.

27. Wayne Muller, *Sabbath: Finding Rest, Renewal, and Delight in Our Busy Lives* (New York: Bantam Books, 1999), 51.

28. Muller, 50.

29. Rabbi Abraham Ben-Isaiah and Rabbi Benjamin Sharfman, *The Pentateuch and Rashi's Commentary: A Linear Translation into English—Exodus* (Brooklyn, NY: S.S. & R. Publishing Company, Inc., 1977), 396.

30. David L. Lieber, senior ed., *Etz Hayim: Torah and Commentary* (New York: The Jewish Publication Society, 2001), 529.

31. Ringwald, 53.

32. Ronald A. Heifetz and Marty Linsky, *Leadership on the Line: Staying Alive through the Dangers of Leading* (Boston: Harvard Business School Press, 2002), 204.

33. Heifetz, Linsky, 204.

·3·

spirituality and spiritual practices

CHAPTER 2 MADE the case for taking time apart as an essential strategy for leadership effectiveness. In this context, effectiveness speaks to the leader's ability to foster a generative capacity, where the congregation or organization continually assesses its work for opportunities to improve and adaptively respond to new challenges. Such leadership requires time apart for reflection because it helps the leader gain perspective on the demands of the environment. But are there activities or practices that promote such reflection? Chapter 3 responds to this question by considering the topic of spirituality. It is in considering the purpose of reflection that we find great overlap and commonality with spirituality.

Spirituality is a common human experience. All human beings exercise spirituality as a means of orienting their lives toward an ideal. That process of orientation is accomplished through engaging patterned actions or spiritual practices. Therefore, this chapter will consider various spiritual practices and their applications. This review demonstrates that, as leaders engage spiritual practices, they are able to cultivate an inner life and in doing so, realize effectiveness in their leadership.

The Case for Reflection

If one of our goals as pastoral leaders is to be effective, and if effectiveness increases by engaging in time apart for reflection and renewal, it follows that we should take time apart to realize effectiveness. What remains open for consideration, however, is whether or not specific acts enhance our ability to be reflective and, as such, do they serve to make time apart more effective. If so, what are these acts?

Consider the intent of reflection: to search for meaning and purpose beyond ourselves. Moreover, through the reflection, we orient our lives by adopting and adapting practices, rituals, and behaviors to help us achieve or move toward an ultimate perceived value.[1] This, according to author and educator Sandra Schneiders, is the definition of spirituality. Spirituality is a lived experience that can be defined as conscious, reflective involvement in the project of life-integration through self-transcendence toward the ultimate value one perceives.[2]

More simply put, through the exercise of spirituality, we attempt to make sense of our lives, reconciling our experiences and determining goals in order to reach some ultimate ideal. In this regard, spirituality is an exercise common to everyone. All of us endeavor to orient our lives toward some desired, ultimate end or purpose, based on past experiences and future desires. This is a universal human trait and characteristic; therefore, spirituality is a basic human quality.

The Commonality of Spirituality

This foundation is important in determining how we apply spirituality. It is the lived experience of spirituality—that is, how individuals actually exercise spirituality—which needs to be understood to determine whether or not the use or application of particular practices fosters growth toward a determined and desired ideal.

At the same time, our understanding needs to make space for an interpretation of spirituality that could be secular or religious. I am decidedly Christian, which introduces recognized biases. However, I also acknowledge that viewing spirituality from a wider frame is consistent with the notion of spirituality encompassing all aspects of being human and supplying a means of experiencing life.[3] This viewpoint is in keeping with an increasingly pluralistic and secular culture in which spirituality does not necessarily hold a religious connotation. For many, spirituality is individualistic, unique, and unattached to religion.

Nevertheless, I agree with researchers Young and Koopsen, who suggest "no discussion of spirituality would be complete without referring to the concept of a Higher Power or creator."[4] As Christians, our spirituality acknowledges the God of Abraham and Sarah as the ultimate concern of our lives, is modeled after the life of Jesus Christ, and is identified with the Holy Spirit.

We exercise or engage our spirituality by patterning our lives after the life, death, and resurrection of Jesus Christ, while being led and guided by the power of the Holy Spirit as a means to wholeness in God. However, as noted above, it is the individual who determines the ultimate end after which a spiritual life is patterned. The patterned actions undertaken by the individual enable each of us to realize a desired end state. What, then, are these patterned actions?

Role of Spiritual Disciplines

As noted in the previous chapter, Jesus engaged in prayer during his time apart. Prayer is just one example of a spiritual discipline that can help us cultivate a spiritual life. Just as Jesus used prayer to place himself before God so he might find direction in decision making, relief in times of stress, and renewal for his soul, spiritual disciplines allow us to place ourselves before God so that God can transform us,[5] providing us with the instruction that we need. Thus, our intent as we engage in spiritual disciplines is transformation. As we engage in the disciplines, we gain experience and that experience helps us realize our transformation.

Taken together, spiritual disciplines not only speak to the act of intentionally bringing our lived spirituality into a conscious realm in order to encounter God, but they also transform us to realize growth and understanding. In her book *Soul Feast*, Marjorie Thompson likens spiritual disciplines to garden tools.[6] Just as use of the best spade or hoe does not alone promise a good crop, the application of spiritual disciplines does not in itself guarantee spiritual maturation. However, the spiritual disciplines *can* foster and facilitate unobstructed, healthy growth. Spiritual disciplines make us receptive to God's love, which in turn yields fruit in our lives.

Moreover, spiritual practices help us to make space for God in our world. This is where the notion of discipline, as in rigorous training, takes shape. According to author Tony Jones, through spiritual disciplines, "we make less of ourselves so that we can be more aware of what God is up to."[7] This only happens as we practice the disciplines. It is reminiscent of the apostle Paul who wrote of an athletic competition (1 Corinthians 9:25). Athletes exercise self-control in order to receive a perishable wreath. As Paul urged the Corinthian Christians, we are called to train our minds and bodies so we are aligned with God's divine will for our lives.

Richard Foster, in his book *Celebration of Discipline*, identifies classical disciplines as those that are central to experiential Christianity. For Foster, inward disciplines include meditation, prayer, fasting, and study; outward disciplines include simplicity, solitude, submission, and service; and corporate disciplines include confession, worship, guidance, and celebration.[8] Inward disciplines cultivate an inner spiritual life because they require introspection and personal examination. Outward disciplines prepare us to extend ourselves to others in order to serve the greater good. Corporate disciplines unite us in community and bring us closer to God and one another.

Like Foster, Tony Jones, in his book *The Sacred Way*, offers categorizations that divide spiritual practices into contemplative approaches versus bodily approaches. The contemplative approaches include silence, sacred reading, prayer, meditation, Ignatian Examen, icons, and spiritual direction. Bodily approaches include the labyrinth, stations of the cross, pilgrimage, fasting, signs of the cross, sabbath, and service.

Marjorie Thompson does not offer categorizations, but simply lists practices that serve generally as an invitation to the Christian spiritual life. She highlights spiritual reading, prayer, worship, fasting, examination, spiritual direction, and hospitality as practices that provide nourishment for parched souls. By nurturing the inner life, individuals discover a positive impact in the ways they relate to others, make decisions, and spend resources. In short, our inner preparation through spiritual practice readies us for outward action. By experiencing the living bread and waters of spiritual disciplines, we can lead others to similarly partake.[9]

In *Practicing Our Faith: A Way of Life for a Searching People*, Dorothy C. Bass explores the practices of honoring the body, hospitality, household economics, keeping sabbath, saying yes and saying no, discernment, testimony, shaping communities, forgiveness, healing, dying well, and singing our lives to God.[10] She also collaborates with thirteen authors in *On Our Way: Christian Practices for Living a Whole Life*, exploring different spiritual practices that conspire to help each individual live a whole life attentively together in the real world for the good of all in response to God. Those practices include study, discerning God's call, living as community, friendship and intimacy, singing, caring for creation, making a good living, honoring the body, knowing and loving our neighbors of other faiths, peacemaking and nonviolence, doing justice, and living in the presence of God.[11]

This survey clearly identifies a multitude of spiritual practices. In sorting through the array of practices, however, we find no definitive list of spiritual disciplines. As Perrin notes, spiritual practice is a fluid term that refers to a large variety of activities in relationship to Christian spirituality.[12] Indeed, a variety of authors cite diverse spiritual practices from art,[13] strategic planning,[14] and leadership[15] to multiculturalism.[16] This diversity notwithstanding, several general points can be concluded with regard to spiritual practices or disciplines.

1. Spiritual practices incorporated into our lives are personal choices. Because we self-select the ideal to which we model our lives, the practices selected to help us reach that ideal will necessarily vary. Meditation might be the most effective way for me to connect to God, but someone else may prefer reading Scriptures to hear God through the Word.

2. Spiritual practices are intentional activities that help us deepen our relationship to the Divine.[17] While the Divine to which we aspire differs, the process is similar. One individual who identifies a personal God as her ideal may cite prayer as the means to connect to that ideal. Another who identifies the spirituality of nature as his ideal may cite a walk in the woods to connect to that ideal. In either case,

the practice enables the individual to draw closer to his or her ideal.

3. The application of spiritual practices is a process. We need to have a vision of our ultimate end or aim. Then we must identify what must change in us to realize our aim, select and implement practices in keeping with our aim, and experiment as we reflect on whether or not progress is realized.[18] We undergo an implied trial and error process to identify practices that will be most effective for us.

4. We grow artfully as spiritual practices require the contribution of all levels of our person.[19] As we engage fully, we will realize the greatest resonance with a practice and, in doing so, experience the greatest growth.

These points are consistent with Daniel Goleman's model of self-directed learning, which involves five discoveries that serve as a tool, enabling individuals to most effectively develop or strengthen an aspect of their ideal self.[20] These discoveries are, in order:

+ My ideal self —Who do I want to be?
+ My real self—Who am I? What are my strengths and gaps?
+ My learning agenda—How can I build on my strengths while reducing my gaps?
+ Experimenting with and practicing new behaviors, thoughts, and feelings to the point of mastery.
+ Developing supportive and trusting relationships that make change possible.[21]

While Goleman's process does not explicitly speak of spiritual practices, the intentional act of incorporating new behaviors in an effort to realize an ideal self is the basis for employing spiritual practices. Goleman acknowledges how to realize efficacy: individuals undergo a process to change in sustainable ways and realize a desired effect. To that end, spiritual practices help individuals to grow toward an ideal.

Specific spiritual practices also yield recognized benefits. Prayer, for example, is considered a means of grace because through prayer, we grow in our appreciation of God as we become attuned to the presence and move of God in our lives. Additionally, through our prayer the peace of God guards our hearts and minds (Philippians

4:7). Thus, prayer yields a sense of peace. In fact, the biblical example provides a compelling witness for the power of prayer. Through prayer, people are healed (Genesis 20:17; Psalm 30:2), battles are won (Exodus 17:8-13; 1 Samuel 7:7-12), hearts are changed (1 Kings 18:36-39; Nehemiah 1:1-2:8), and blessings are bestowed (Genesis 49:22-26; Matthew 14:19).

Contemplative practices such as meditation provide individuals with the experience of inscape, which enables the individual to look inwardly and consider the deep reality of things to find God, meaning, and sustenance.[22] The spiritual practice of fasting is commended to help us keep balance in life, increase effectiveness in intercessory prayer, provide guidance in decisions, and promote physical well-being, among other things.[23] The practice of study increases a sense of mindfulness and helps individuals to be more attentive to life.[24] Ignatius developed the spiritual exercises, which are a compilation of practices offered to help individuals become self-conquering through the examination of conscience in order to seek and find divine will.

Yet, what these benefits have in common is that they are qualitative in nature, with benefits that are arguably subjective. Such subjectivity has traditionally caused researches to denigrate reported benefits of spiritual practices because of the inherent inability to "approach scientifically something so ineffable, intangible, and mysterious as religious experience."[25] However, attitudes have begun to shift as studies demonstrate the quantifiable benefits of spiritual practices. Spirituality and spiritual practices are sentimental niceties no longer, given the large body of serious academic literature written on the positive influences of the spirituality-health relationship.[26] Research on the connection between spirituality and health demonstrates:

+ Persons who attend religious services regularly (once a week or more) are only about half as likely to be depressed as those who do not attend services;[27]
+ Many people depend on religion and spirituality as their primary method of coping with physical health problems and the stress of surgery;[28]
+ People who regularly attend religious services have lower rates of illness and death than do infrequent or non-attenders;[29]

✦ For each of the three leading causes of death in the United States—heart disease, cancer, and hypertension—people who report a religious affiliation have lower rates of illness.[30]

✦ Even after the availability of antiretroviral therapy, people living with HIV/AIDS often relied on religiousness and spirituality to cope with their disease.[31]

These are overall findings about the role of religious and spiritual factors. However, researchers have also reported detailed findings about the application of specific spiritual practices. For example, studies show that meditation reduces the body's response (sweat) level, breath rate, and blood measures.[32] Meditation is also credited with decreasing the frequency of irregular heart rhythms and reducing cholesterol levels.[33] Studies on the use of the Eight-Point Program of Passage Meditation, a process that features the contemplative practices of meditation and mantra repetition, have produced positive empirical evidence of reduced stress, increased ability to focus on the task at hand, a renewed sense of enjoyment in work, and better emotional balance.[34]

With regard to the practice of prayer, studies show those who pray have lower blood pressure, decreased depression, and a better ability to cope with stress.[35] A 2001 study in Egypt found that 60 percent of patients undergoing an MRI examination spontaneously used prayer to relieve anxiety.

The aforementioned studies focused on patient healthcare outcomes related to spirituality. However, healthcare leaders have themselves been the focus of studies that consider the benefits of spiritual practices. In one such study, researchers surveyed nurse leaders to determine the effects of a four-week mindfulness meditation course in stress management.[36] In the study, nurses were taught mindfulness based stress reduction (MBSR) principles as a means to deepen the capacity for attention and strengthen present-moment awareness.[37] Studies have demonstrated that by training the mind through meditative disciplines such as MBSR, individuals can grow into seeing more clearly and acting spontaneously with greater awareness, compassion, and wisdom.[38] The nursing profession is a high-stress occupation, and stress may impair a leader's ability to communicate effectively, make decisions, and inspire others. Thus, mindfulness was conceptualized as a way of helping nurse leaders care for and nurture themselves. The results of the study demonstrated that by learning to be fully present with oneself through mindfulness practices, the nurse leader was more caring and effective for others by extension.[39]

This study was not unique. More than one thousand research studies have appeared in various professional publications attempting to establish a connection among spirituality, religious factors, and health. Even so, limited evidence serves to establish a link between spirituality and health.[40] At issue is the difficulty of designing a study where the variables can be controlled in a consistent and repeatable manner. An individual's spiritual experience may exhibit a different outcome if the study were conducted at a different time or under different circumstances.

Nevertheless, even subjective experiences seem to explain the explosion of spirituality and the practice of spiritual disciplines in leadership. And because of the chaotic and sometimes stressful nature of leadership, authors such as Bill George suggest that individuals require personal time to relieve tension and manage the stress created by leadership roles.[41] Leaders whom George surveyed commended such spiritual practices as prayer, meditation, spiritual reading, and taking sabbaticals. To be fair, other practices such as exercise, time with friends, listening to music, or watching television were offered as stress relievers as well.

George argued that it mattered less which practices were engaged, and more that there was some routine by which an individual managed stress and had time to think clearly about life, work, and personal issues.[42] Such practices, whether or not their roots were spiritual, served as strategies through which leaders were able to restore themselves and regain perspective in order to remain grounded, integrated, and true to their authentic self.[43]

Clearly, spiritual practices employed for such purposes are strategies for self-care, helping leaders fight against burnout. Stress has a wearing affect, causing us to become narrower in thinking, less open to new possibilities, and seemingly victimized by circumstances beyond individual control.[44] Thus, it follows that we need a variety of strategies that will help combat and overcome the effects of stress. Specifically, practices that help us let go of attitudes of indispensability, relax and play, set boundaries, nurture relationships, engage the spirit, invigorate the body, increase learning, and encourage reflection provide helpful handles on the discipline of self-care.[45]

Engaging spiritual practices for the purpose of self-care is one possible application in leadership. However, spiritual practices are also used by leaders to guide and direct them in leadership. When ministers withdraw to connect or reconnect with God's call on their lives, they are better prepared for the work necessary to bring God's vision to fruition. The practice of stepping away to center on our image of the ideal not only represents the exercise of spirituality, but also offers the opportunity to discover or rediscover our purpose.

Discernment is another practice for leadership, increasingly being used in decision making to help leaders determine directions that have staying power. Studies of senior managers' decisions show half of the decisions made are no longer in effect after two years.[46] Discernment combats such high rates of decision failure by providing deeper consideration of possible directions and outcomes. Discernment intentionally focuses on God's will to help us sense where God's Spirit is leading. Discernment may involve individuals, small groups, and the whole organization in a process of prayer, reflection, consideration of the questions at hand, and careful listening.

By sifting through interior and exterior experiences, we can distinguish between God's call versus those experiences that pull us away from God. Such a process allows us to expand understanding, identify options, and cut through distractions and attachments to gain a clearer perspective of reality.

As leaders engage in spiritual practices, their leadership is positively impacted. In her book *Soul at Work*, Margaret Benefiel interviewed "spiritually grounded leaders" (those who regularly engage in individual and communal spiritual practices) in order to understand how such leaders act in various situations. Through her interviews, Benefiel noted these leaders exhibited strong listening skills, empowered others, operated with integrity, remained deeply grounded in the midst of turmoil, demonstrated compassion, and valued relationships.[47] These common attributes were the product of different spiritual practices.

These spiritually grounded leaders cultivated an inner life that they brought to bear in positive ways on their organizations, resulting in better organizational health and overall success. This observation demonstrates the insight that "Leadership effectiveness will be shaped not by playing the right roles, but by embodying the right qualities."[48] And it is the exercise of spiritual practices that helps individuals develop the right qualities. Bill Easum's contention summarizes this point nicely: "Everything I know about leadership screams for us to go as deep in our spirituality as is possible, to be more and do less."[49]

While the benefits of spiritual practices remain difficult to quantify based on the challenges of correlating the application of spirituality to measurable outcomes, I contend that quantifying the outcome is not important. Rather, we want to understand the lived experience of those who engage in spiritual practices while taking time apart in the midst of leadership. What is their experience and how might those experiences inform us? As David Perrin notes, "the content of lived experience is the object of inquiry in spirituality . . . ; we need to find a way to get at this lived experience to give it shape."[50]

This was my desire: to get at the lived experience by exploring and understanding what happens as pastoral leaders engage in spiritual practices, having separated themselves from their leadership context. What I discovered was a correlation. As leaders took time apart, they engaged in practices that helped them better align with their ideal. Subsequently, leaders were able to return to their leadership contexts, having been renewed and prepared to reengage. In short, they were made more effective in their leadership through engagement in spiritual practices.

Part One of this book has dealt with theory that supports the hypothesis that leaders who take time apart from their leadership context in order to engage in spiritual practices are more effective. However, we need more than theory. Each of us can read a compelling argument but never really put it into practice. Therefore, I want to provide the practical application to make it possible for pastoral leaders to incorporate this process and realize leadership effectiveness in daily life.

That is what the 7 Rs of Sanctuary does. It provides a process to encourage you to step away from your place of leadership in order to expansively reflect. In doing so, the process helps you realize leadership effectiveness and well-being in support of your ministry. The process is detailed in Part Two.

NOTES

1. David B. Perrin, *Studying Christian Spirituality* (New York: Routledge, 2007), 19.
2. Sandra M. Schneiders, "The Study of Christian Spirituality: Contours and Dynamics of a Discipline," *Minding the Spirit: The Study of Christian Spirituality*, ed. Elizabeth A. Dreyer and Mark S. Burrows (Baltimore: John Hopkins University Press, 2005), 5–6.
3. Caroline Young and Cyndie Koopsen, *Spirituality, Health and Healing* (Thorofare, NJ: Slack Inc., 2005), 4.
4. Young and Koopsen, 4.
5. Richard J. Foster, *Celebration of Discipline: The Path to Spiritual Growth* (New York: HarperCollins, 1998), 7.
6. Marjorie J. Thompson, *Soul Feast: An Invitation to the Christian Spiritual Life* (Louisville: Westminster John Knox Press, 2005), 10.
7. Tony Jones, *The Sacred Way: Spiritual Practices for Everyday Life* (Grand Rapids: Zondervan, 2005), 32.
8. Foster, 1.
9. Thompson, 17.
10. Dorothy C. Bass, ed., *Practicing Our Faith: A Way of Life for a Searching People* (San Francisco: Jossey-Bass, 1997), vii–viii.
11. Dorothy C. Bass and Susan R. Briehl, eds., *On Our Way: Christian Practices for Living a Whole Life* (Nashville: Upper Room Books, 2010), 13–16.
12. Perrin, 266.
13. Robert Wuthnow, "Art as Spiritual Practice," *Creative Spirituality: The Way of the Artist* (Berkeley: University of California Press, 2001), 107–38.
14. Gil Rendle and Alice Mann, *Holy Conversations: Strategic Planning as a Spiritual Practice for Congregations* (Bethesda, MD: Alban Institute, 2003), 23.
15. Anthony B. Robinson, "Give and Take: Leadership as a Spiritual Practice," *Christian Century*, October 4, 2005, 28–32.
16. Elizabeth Conde-Frazier, S. Steve Kang, and Gary A. Parret, *A Many-Colored Kingdom: Multicultural Dynamics for Spiritual Formation* (Grand Rapids, MI: Baker Academic, 2004), 167–210.
17. Evan B. Howard, *The Brazos Introduction to Christian Spirituality* (Grand Rapids, MI: Baker Publishing Company, 2008), 281.
18. Howard, 282.
19. Perrin, 266.
20. Daniel Goleman, Richard Boyatzis, and Annie McKee, *Primal Leadership: Learning to Lead with Emotional Intelligence* (Boston: Harvard Business School Press, 2004), 109.
21. Goleman, Boyatzis, and McKee, 111–12.
22. Thomas Ryan, *Prayer of Heart & Body: Meditation and Yoga as Christian Spiritual Practice* (Mahwah, NJ: Paulist Press, 1995), 61.
23. Foster, 56.
24. Matthew Myer Boulton, "Study," *On Our Way: Christian Practices for Living a Whole Life*, eds. Dorothy C. Bass and Susan R. Briehl (Nashville: Upper Room Books, 2010), 25–26.
25. Thomas G. Plante and Allen C. Sherman, "Research on Faith and Health: New Approaches to Old Questions," *Faith and Health: Psychological Perspectives*, eds. Thomas G. Plante and Allen C. Sherman (New York: The Guilford Press, 2001), 2.
26. Perrin, 305.

27. P. S. Mueller, D. J. Plevak, and T. A. Rummans, "Religious Involvement, Spirituality and Medicine: Implications for Clinical Practice," *Mayo Clinic Proceedings* 2001, 76: 1225–35.

28. E. D. Boudreaux, E. O'Hea, and R. Chasuk, "Spiritual Role in Healing: An Alternative Way of Thinking," *Primary Care: Clinics in Office Practice* 2002; 29(2): 439–54.

29. Jeff Levin, *God, Faith and Health: Exploring the Spirituality-Healing Connection* (New York: John Wiley & Sons, 2001), 3.

30. Levin, 3.

31. K. A. Lorenz, R. D. Hays, M. F. Shapiro, P. D. Cleary, S. M. Asch, and N. S. Wenger, "Religiousness and Spirituality among HIV-infected Americans," *Journal of Palliative Medicine* 2005, 8: 774–81.

32. Ryan, 88.

33. Ryan, 199.

34. Tim Flinders, Doug Oman, and Carol Lee Flinders, "The Eight-Point Program of Passage Meditation: Health Effects of a Comprehensive Program," *Spirit, Science and Health: How the Spiritual Mind Fuels Physical Wellness*, eds. Thomas G. Plante and Carl E. Thoresen (Westport, CT: Praeger Publishers, 2007), 72–85.

35. Howard, 324.

36. Teri Britt Pipe, Jennifer J. Bortz, and Amylou Dueck, "Nurse Leader Mindfulness Meditation Program for Stress Management: A Randomized Controlled Trial," *The Journal of Nursing Administration*, March 2009, Volume 39, No. 3: 130.

37. Britt Pipe, Bortz, Dueck, 131.

38. Bob Stahl and Elisha Goldstein, *A Mindfulness-Based Stress Reduction Workbook* (Oakland, CA: New Harbinger Publications, Inc., 2010), xi.

39. J. Watson, *Postmodern Nursing and Beyond* (Edinburgh, Scotland: Churchill-Livingstone/Harcourt-Brace, 1999).

40. Carl E. Thoresen, "Spirituality, Religion, and Health: What's the Deal?" *Spirit, Science and Health: How the Spiritual Mind Fuels Wellness*, eds. Thomas G. Plante and Carl E. Thoresen (Westport, CT: Praeger, 2007), 7.

41. Bill George, *True North: Discover Your Authentic Leadership* (San Francisco: Jossey-Bass, 2007), 144.

42. George, 144.

43. George, 141.

44. Jeffrey D. Jones, *Heart, Mind and Strength: Theory and Practice for Congregational Leadership* (Herndon, VA: Alban Institute, 2008), 40.

45. J Jones, 43.

46. Paul Nutt, "Surprising but True: Half the Decisions in Organizations Fail," *Academy of Management Executive* 13 (1999): 75–90.

47. Margaret Benefiel, *Soul at Work: Spiritual Leadership in Organizations* (New York: Seabury Books, 2005), 51.

48. Jeffrey D. Jones, "Leading for the Future" *Congregations* 2006, Volume 32, No. 1: 15.

49. Bill Easum, *Leadership on the Other Side: No Rules, Just Clues* (Nashville: Abington Press, 2000), 126.

50. Perrin, 49.

⋆ PART TWO ⋆
introducing the 7 Rs
of santuary

PART ONE OF this book sought to answer the question of leadership effectiveness from the perspective of leadership theory, religious tradition, and applied practices in spirituality. Beyond these findings, however, I wanted to understand from ministry leaders whether taking time apart and engaging in spiritual practices—a process I call sanctuary—results in leadership effectiveness.

By virtue of my own experience, I know full well the challenges of leadership. Having been a chief operating officer, chief information officer, senior pastor, and now executive director, I recognize the demands placed on leaders to ensure organizational success. Moreover, I know the stressors that arise in uncertain environments and how easy it is to get caught up in a swirling tide of anxious momentum. Therefore, I know the need for strategies to help pastoral leaders realize efficacy in their leadership. Recognizing my call to serve pastoral leaders, I have attempted to identify such strategies so that I might share them with others.

The leaders with whom I spoke desire the best for their congregations and organizations. Their responses clearly conveyed their desires to be their most effective selves, and they were committed to helping others realize the same efficacy.

They do this by engaging in sanctuary. Specifically and without exception, every leader could share experiences where he or she intentionally stepped away from their leadership context for physical and mental time apart. That time apart has been absolutely critical for allowing them to slow down and disconnect. Leaders needed time to allow their minds to settle, to break away from the complexities of their leadership, and to simply be dormant. Time apart achieves this.

Yet, time apart is not enough. We have each had the experience of getting away for a weekend, only to return on Monday morning no better prepared to deal with the workday challenges than when we left on Friday afternoon. What makes the difference is the ability to step back and view things from a distance in order to create perspective.

Stepping back is an exercise in creating objectivity, and reflection during that time apart becomes the most significant activity undertaken to increase objectivity. The act of reflection makes it possible for leaders to regain a sense of purpose, determine what needs to be done, and return to their leadership context ready to re-engage. The ability to reflect on an action and learn from it helps us manage the dynamics of a changing environment. Reflection is the core capability for leadership effectiveness because it helps sharpen our focus as we attempt to mobilize and motivate others.

Through reflection and other self-selected spiritual practices, ministry leaders saw themselves approach their ideal selves. These leaders perceived such patterned actions, specifically in the form of spiritual practices, as spiritually significant. And as these leaders engaged in practices such as meditation, prayer, study, silence, and worship, which cultivated their inner life, they were ultimately readied for outward action.

The lived experiences of these pastoral leaders suggest that leadership theorists who commend taking time apart to reflect do not go far enough; even the concept of sanctuary as Heifetz defines it is insufficient. We need an expanded definition of sanctuary, one that encompasses the act of taking time apart for the express purpose of engaging in spiritual practices. Reflection, prayer, meditation, or walking in the woods—all these practices and more yielded efficacy for the leaders with whom I spoke. This combination of actions allowed them to cultivate their inner spiritual lives, while regaining a sense of self, and preparing them to return to their leadership context ready to reengage.

My conversations highlighted other benefits as well. Leaders spoke of increased well-being in terms of calm, peace, confidence, and certainty as a result of sanctuary. They expected engagement to yield beneficial outcomes and found it was more than simply selecting a desired practice. The most critical experience was an intentional exercise of a practice.

This characteristic of intentionality parallels Jesus' intentional practices of daily withdrawal and retreat. Clearly, Jesus exercised control during his times of engagement and disengagement in the course of his leadership. Thus, each individual should embrace the freedom to select the practices most meaningful for that leader. Rather than dictate specific practices, individuals must adopt and adapt whatever practices will allow them to reach their desired ideal.

What I learned from these pastoral leaders moves me to offer a strategy to help leaders intentionally take time apart to engage in spiritual practices to realize effectiveness in pastoral leadership. I wanted to create a flexible process that could be used daily, weekly, or for extended time periods. The process provides space for leaders to exercise spirituality in keeping with their individual needs and goals. I determined that the process needed to allow for physical and mental separation from one's leadership context. It needed to enable the leader to disconnect from the challenges of their environment and feature reflection as a primary activity. As part of the exercise of reflection, the process needed to make it possible for the leader to consider and select outcomes, readying them to return to their leadership context refreshed.

The 7 Rs of Sanctuary

I call the process the 7 Rs of Sanctuary.

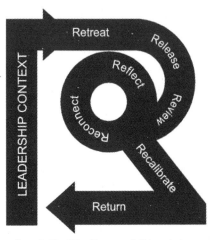

Figure 1 - The 7 Rs of Sanctuary © Debora Jackson

Retreat—The first step in the process is to retreat intentionally from your leadership context. An isolated physical space is necessary whereby a leader can create separation from the work and its challenges.

Release—Second, having achieved some degree of physical distance, you must mentally release from the leadership environment. Release provides the opportunity to slow down and to engage in a period of dormancy—to *be* rather than *do*.

Review—Third, review your current leadership context. Do this in a mindful way, considering without condemnation and allowing thoughts to flow like clouds drifting by. Consider, what is going well? What could be improved? Are you where you hoped to be?

Reconnect—In this fourth step, reconnect to the ideals that are core to who you are and where you are going. Mindfully remember and then rekindle the flame of dreams lost. Consider your goals and your plans to make them a reality.

Reflect—Fifth is the critical task of reflection. Look at your current context and the situation you remembered during review. Then, look back to examine the original goals and ideals that came to mind during reconnection. Hold those ideas in parallel to recognize the gaps and disconnects.

Recalibrate—The sixth step selects from the specific actions and approaches that emerge to create an opportunity to mentally try it on for size. Focus on emerging plans and strategies to sense whether you experience energy and excitement from the thought of them. Project each plan and consider it for feasibility. Take the opportunity to rest in the decision to recalibrate your goals and realign your plans as needed.

Return—In this seventh and final step, prepare to return to your leadership context. Take time to appreciate the renewed sense of purpose that has emerged in sanctuary. It is the opportunity to rest in certainty, rejoice in a greater sense of calm and grounding, and get excited about returning with a strategy and plan in mind—or at least be at peace having had the space to engage with your ideal self.

The following chapters explore each of the 7 Rs in turn—the steps by which a leader can take time apart from the leadership context to engage in spiritual practices. I encourage you to experience sanctuary by engaging in the 7 Rs. It will make a difference in your effectiveness as a leader.

·4·

retreat

He said to them, "Come away to a deserted place all by yourselves and rest a while." (Mark 6:31)

WHY DID JESUS invite his disciples to retreat from the work of the ministry? Because Jesus recognized the challenge of the work. He understood how such work requires a time of restoration. Ministry requires retreat.

According to the Gospel of Mark, when Jesus began his ministry, he went out to the villages to preach and teach. He called disciples and sent them out to minister in two-person teams among the people. Their instructions were to go empty-handed to preach and teach, cast out demons, anoint the sick and heal them. The disciples did as Jesus instructed, and many experienced healing because of their ministry.

In short, the disciples' ministry effort was a great success, and it is easy to imagine how energizing such success would have been. Through the disciples' healing touch, people who suffered illness and disease were made well. Because they had been imbued with power over evil spirits, demons fled upon their word and command.

As many ministers can attest, in the excitement of ministry success, no one thinks about taking a break. No one thinks of getting something to eat. No one is concerned about taking a rest. When the success of the moment is so great, bodily needs hardly rate a consideration. When the disciples returned to Jesus, they were clearly excited. But by the same token, it is easy to imagine when they finally slowed down, an inevitable and natural fatigue set in. Perhaps that was when Jesus said, "Come away to a deserted place all by yourselves and rest awhile." Just as Jesus invited his disciples to retreat, pastoral leaders today are urged to accept the invitation to retreat, to step away from their leadership context in order to rest and be renewed.

The Need for Retreat

Depleting Demands of Ministry

The work and demands of the pastorate are endless—caring for the congregation, leading worship, encouraging spiritual deepening, managing the administrative functions of the church, and planning for the future. This work can bring great joy because it is a tremendous privilege and honor to walk with people who find Christ through our ministry. It is exhilarating to be on the journey with people as they realize a deeper relationship with God. It is gratifying when people mature in their faith and become active members of the congregation we serve.

However, the work can also be depleting. For each joyous situation, the demands of ministry create a pull that diminishes the energies of the ministerial leader. First, pastors are expected to be "on" at a moment's notice. An innocent conversation may quickly turn into the need for pastoral care. A social situation for anyone else—a cup of coffee shared after worship, a chance meeting in the parking lot of a local market, or the innocent inquiry about the family—becomes cause for further care and concern. Such needs do not present themselves at neat, tidy times, and while the timing may be inconvenient, these are moments when ministry happens. As such, the pastor puts aside personal needs to respond to the needs of others.

Second, depletion occurs because there is an inherent imbalance in the role of the pastor. At times, pastoral ministry is reduced to that of a hireling: one who is expected to be responsible or accountable in any given situation. If a community meeting occurs during the day, people assume the pastor can attend on behalf of the church. After all, "pastors only work on Sundays," or so some people believe. If there is a shortfall in giving, the pastor is expected to address it. If the church property has a need, the pastor is supposed to respond. Other church members may opt to skip a program, offer their regrets for missing a meeting, or simply fail to deliver on a promised assignment, but the pastor does not have this luxury. Pastors are expected to deliver and live up to the standards of others, no matter how unfair the burden may be.

It is not solely congregational expectations that deplete the pastor; pastoral leaders struggle with their own unrealistic expectations about how they should spend their time and fulfill their ministry responsibilities. Believing the most important work of ministry is accomplished through relationships, pastors tend to invest a lot of energy in relational tasks, such as visiting the sick or performing community outreach. In contrast, administrative tasks such as follow-up phone calls, email correspondence, meeting preparation, and strategic planning are lower priorities. Often, pastors squeeze those duties into the margins of available time or, even worse, during what should be family or personal time.

For too many pastors, personal needs are the lowest priority, which means the time for prayer, meditation, or Bible study is virtually nonexistent. This is not because pastors think themselves above the need for prayer and study time. Rather, it is an endemic belief that the pastor must take care of others first. As a result, personal spiritual deepening and nurture rarely happen with the kind of frequency required for sustaining ministry. In fact, many pastors acknowledge that the only time they open their Bible is when preparing their weekly sermon.

Loss of Self

Pastors are at risk of losing themselves because of depleting demands. Not only is loss of self a risk in the face of ministry pressures, but it is a risk in the face of ministry joys. Consider again the narrative in Mark 6, when Jesus sent the disciples out to minister in pairs, telling them to take no additional provisions for their journeys—no extra tunic or shoes, no food or staff, and no money.

Needless to say, the disciples were dubious about these directives. How were they to provide for themselves? What was supposed to happen while they were out on the road doing ministry? Nevertheless, they did as Jesus instructed and went forth.

What they experienced was nothing short of miraculous—not only in what they accomplished but in how everything they needed was provided. They were so excited about what had occurred that they wanted to continue to revel in the experience. Even though they had been ministering nonstop, they wanted to continue to share. They were ready to continue working, ignoring their human needs because the joys of ministry had been so great.

Ministry is filled with both joys and challenges, and both can drive us to denial when we don't take time to eat or rest, to study or play, to invest in our family or self.

Once I asked one of the church deacons to accompany me on several visits to those who were hospitalized or homebound. We went from nursing home to hospital to residential home—never stopping for a break, with no water and no food. I thought nothing of the pace. In fact, I was elated to have visited so many people. Only later did the deacon confide in others that she was hesitant about accompanying me on future visitations. She remembered feeling thirsty and hungry and wanting to take a break, but I never seemed to stop.

In hindsight I recognize my pace was not healthy. When we give so much of ourselves to the work, an inevitable blurring occurs and the distinction between the self and the role is lost. In the case of too many pastors, we are no longer *in ministry*. We become *the minister*, taking on the expectation that "I am the role and the role is me." While this is a noble stance, it is also potentially abusive to the leader because as the individual self is lost, the spirit withers. Without time to be replenished, the self starts to withdraw and contract. No one can be "on" all the time. We each need time when we are simply a child of God without the expectation to deliver.

The outcome of such blurring is the inability to function in healthy and effective ways. When there is no distinction between self and the role, leading is more difficult as well. We become subject to our environment, which impacts our ability to discern possible options because we are too close to the situation to make the best decisions. People need distance to realize perspective, and perspective provides the impetus for creativity. When we are too close to a situation, or when we can no longer separate ourselves from our roles, our proximity clouds our vision. In our limited capacity, we have a high potential for mistakes, and our decisions can be shortsighted.

How do we break the cycle? A change is needed. Jesus said to the disciples, "Come away to a deserted place all by yourselves and rest a while." Come and retreat.

What Is Retreat?

Retreat is an *invitation*. It is an invitation to step away from the rigors and challenges of ministry. Retreat is an invitation to come away and rest. For the minister, it is the invitation to experience ministry in relationship with Jesus Christ by God through the Holy Spirit. It is the invitation to be ministered to rather than to minister.

Retreat is also an *opportunity*. It is the opportunity to take time apart and make space to regain perspective. It is opportunity for the leader to find that isolated physical or mental space where we can create separation from the work and the challenges we confront. Retreat provides each leader with opportunity to seek that deserted place and create time and space for self.

Retreat is also *recognition*. It is the recognition that we need rest. In the midst of ministry, it is too easy to continue to press in hopes of completing the tasks in front of us. There is always one more thing to be done. But we are called to recognize the need for rest. Retreat acknowledges that each of us needs to rest physically and mentally from the work environment. By creating distance between the person and the work, we acknowledge that we need rest.

Again, I think of the disciples returning from their ministries. I imagine everyone bursting through the doorway of their gathering place, creating a cacophony of sounds as everyone excitedly tries to tell the others what they experienced.

"I healed a little girl!" one exclaimed.

"I was praying and a demon left the body of a man," said another.

Others described how strangers provided them with food, clothing, or money because they were recognized as ministers of God. I am sure they were all trying to get to Jesus, saying, "Listen to me," because they were so excited.

Jesus did not entertain any of the euphoric excitement, however. He simply said, "Come and rest." In that moment, what they had done was not important. The excitement they wanted to share was not important. What was important was to change the pace—to break from what had been, to step away and rest. This is, at its heart, the invitation, opportunity, and recognition for retreat.

Scriptural Grounding for Retreat

In Matthew 11:28-29, Jesus said, "Come to me, all you that are weary and are carrying heavy burdens, and I will give you rest. Take my yoke upon you, and learn from me; for I am gentle and humble in heart, and you will find rest for your souls." This is the invitation and opportunity to retreat. We are invited to come—come apart, come away, come from our labors to be with the Lord.

Jesus was trying to show us a different way of being—a way not frenzied or frenetic but a way that is gentle and unhurried. This is what we learn if we accept his invitation. Jesus' way and model of ministry was one in which he ebbed and flowed—from ministry to solitary communion with God—so while he gave of himself, he was never far from his source and supply. That connection made ministry possible. In emptying himself, Jesus was restored and re-fueled to continue to give to others. This is what Jesus is teaching us.

What's more, Jesus is teaching us in a corrective way as he invites us to shoulder his yoke. On one hand, a yoke is clearly a restraint, put in place to constrain and contain. On the other hand, a yoke provides boundaries that keep us grounded and prevent us from straying too far or harming ourselves in the process. By taking on Jesus' yoke, we go at his pace, which means we will never get too far ahead of ourselves, that we will not be overly depleted or drained in the process of doing ministry.

How many times have we said to ourselves, "Just one more thing," or "Just a few more minutes," only to find hours later that we are still working? With Jesus' yoke, we are constrained from such self-abuse. By taking on Jesus' yoke, we learn Jesus' way.

Sometimes we need to walk away from our leadership context. Consider the prophet Elijah in 1 Kings 19. After putting to death all of the prophets of Baal, Jezebel swore to put Elijah to death. He feared for his life and fled. In fact, Elijah fled a full day's journey beyond Beer-sheba into the wilderness. The stresses of leadership can be so great we simply need to get away! Retreat is the recognition that we need to get away from the stresses and, sometimes, the fears we encounter.

But notice that when Elijah retreated to the cave, it was there that he was physically and spiritually nourished. The angel of the Lord came to Elijah and provided food that strengthened and sustained him for 40 days. Moreover, after the 40 days God appeared to Elijah, not in the wind, not in the earthquake, not in the fire, but in the still small voice that served to spiritually undergird Elijah.

Have you ever struggled to hear God's voice while in the stresses and strain of ministry? By following Elijah's example, we can take time apart, becoming more in tune with God and discern the Spirit's voice over the cacophony of other sounds and furies that serve only to distract and lead us further from God's influence in our lives.

Consider Mary in Luke 1. The angel of the Lord has appeared to Mary and told her she would have a child even though she was a virgin and did not yet know a man. Undoubtedly, this was a stressful situation for a young teenaged girl. But Mary is also told that her elderly and heretofore barren cousin is six months pregnant. Mary's first response was to affirm the prophecy given to her. Her second response was to immediately leave for the Judean hill country to visit her cousin. Mary needed to leave her current context and retreat to be with her cousin. In this regard, retreat is also the recognition that there are times when we need the counsel of others to help us in our own situations.

Mary's cousin Elizabeth, being significantly older than Mary, was able to understand the stigma of pregnancy—whether from being unable to conceive or from conceiving in an unexpected and miraculous way. And so Mary was able to draw strength and comfort from her cousin, having taken advantage of the opportunity to retreat.

What Pastoral Leaders Say about Retreat

When asked about retreat, ministerial leaders expressed the benefits of stepping away from their leadership context. For example, one pastoral leader spoke of the need for retreat to help him prepare for the high religious holidays. For him, the high holidays require an enormous amount of time for sermon preparation, given the great burden he places on himself to express his thoughts clearly and to reach people meaningfully. His regular practice was to sequester himself at a local seminary and immerse himself in the Holy Book and other volumes about Judaism. Being able to retreat freed him to write. On other occasions, he retreated by going to lunch at the student cafeteria, where he was surrounded by hundreds of people, none of whom he knew and none of whom knew him. He experienced retreat in the anonymity, which allowed him to let his thoughts go and allowed the Spirit to come. It is what he needed to get close to what was inside of him.

Another leader left her home and traveled to a lovely Jesuit center on the Atlantic Ocean, where she had the opportunity to look upon the waters, walk the beach, and see the power of God through nature. For her the physical setting was part of the experience, as was the opportunity to engage with a faith tradition different from her own. Both helped her step away from her own context physically and mentally. And this stepping away was critical because, given the challenges of her ministry, she came to appreciate retreat for its opportunity to distance herself from personal, professional, and work-related challenges. In retreat, she was not the pastor; she was not "on." Rather, she could heed God's call to rest and listen to God's voice during profound moments of silence and prayer.

A third leader spoke of a practice of withdrawing weekly with his staff for prayer. Once a week for 15 minutes prior to lunch, the staff engages in a time of prayer. The pastor especially appreciated the weekly practice of time apart for prayer in community because he recognized his inability to engage in deep worship as a pastor. While the worship experience may be wonderful for others, he lamented that he himself only felt the pressure of working, doing, and leading. Moreover, in his leadership capacity, this minister is on the road almost every weekend preaching, which limits his ability to simply worship. Retreat in community for him is the opportunity to affirm the words of his mantra, that he is a "child of God: found, free, full, and forgiven, and once in awhile, fruitful."

Retreat provides time and space apart. It is "time spent alone," one leader said, in a space where he can physically separate himself from others. Another leader described retreat as the chance to "decouple from what was experienced in the day to day." That practice of retreating makes it possible to "establish boundaries" and get away from the stresses of the job.

These characterizations give the mental image of stepping away and taking a break so there is distance between an individual and his or her leadership context. It is reminiscent of author Ronald Heifetz's concept of getting on the balcony. In his book *Leadership without Easy Answers*, Heifetz describes the idea to watching dancers on a dance floor. It is impossible to see the patterns of the dance emerge while in the midst of the dancers. But, if we create distance—that is, we ascend to and look down from the balcony—then we can gain greater perspective to see how patterns unfold. The practice of retreat does this for the ministerial leader. By creating time and space apart, we are positioned to engage in the work that lies ahead.

Why Do We Need to Retreat?

As a small child, my son loved hidden picture activities. Hidden picture worksheets feature an ordinary landscape or scene, but within the scene are hidden a number of random objects. The task is to find the camouflaged objects and circle them. Invariably, my son could not find one or two objects. The more he stared at the picture, the more frustrated he became with the task. Too often, what was supposed to be a relaxing pastime ended in frustration with paper and pencils being thrown across the room.

The challenges of pastoral leadership can be like searching for hidden pictures. We stare at a problem or attempt to resolve a situation, but we cannot seem to find the hidden object—the key to make things better. Sometimes we stare at the picture too long and only end up frustrated in the process.

Interestingly, if my husband or I looked over our son's shoulder to help him with the picture, we could quickly find the object that eluded our son. There is a benefit to a fresh set of eyes and a different perspective. And that is the ultimate benefit of retreat. When we take time to retreat, we are able to move on with the day without getting fixated on personal issues. Time apart gives us a renewed sense of perspective, providing courage and resolve to move on in the face of things that create apprehension. Retreat helps us to recognize that staring at and struggling with an issue is an exercise of diminishing returns. We do not become more productive when we wrestle a situation without reprieve. We become more frustrated, and in our frustration, our capacity to resolve a challenge is lessened. In retreat, we step away and discover a break can make all the difference in the world.

I had the opportunity to serve as a retreat leader for the board of a spiritually based organization. As I met with the executive director and planned the retreat with her, she told me the team was available to meet for only 50 minutes of each hour. After 50 minutes, we needed to take a 10-minute break, during which we could not talk about the work we had done. I remember thinking the retreat had no chance of being successful. How would we ever tackle the tough challenges of redefining the organization's mission, vision, and objectives when we only had 50 minutes to use in every hour? My reservations notwithstanding, I acquiesced and led the retreat as instructed.

I was proven completely wrong in my assessment. It was the best retreat ever experienced by the participants and by me as the leader. The meeting had a wonderful rhythm and the attendees seemed to accept and respect that we would only be productive for 50 minutes at a time. The intervals when we took a complete break from the agenda made space for new thoughts and fresh awareness. The experience became for me a clear validation of the need for retreat.

What Can You Do to Retreat?

My retreat leadership example stands as a compelling model for what we need to do in our daily rhythm of work and service. In each hour, we should take a break. What if we made it a habit of working in 50-minute intervals, taking an intentional break to do something completely different? Stand up and stretch; leave the room to get a drink of water; step outside for a breath of fresh air. Each of these simple acts is amazingly beneficial in clearing the mind or invigorating the body.

However, retreat requires more than simply taking a break each hour. One pastor recalled the words of Rick Warren in a radio interview when Warren suggested that every leader take time to divert daily, withdraw weekly, and abandon annually. On a daily basis, we need to step away and divert our attentions and energies from our leadership context.

Several leaders shared that they take a walk daily. It is an opportunity to listen to music, observe the neighborhood, or simply enjoy a change of scenery from where they spend the entire day. I spoke to one pastor who engages in weekly massages. The practice started in response to health concerns because he suffered from scoliosis, curvature of the spine. However, as he underwent this weekly therapy, he came to view it as a form of retreat—an opportunity to get away from the challenges of pastoral ministry and to experience the receiving end of care, rather than being the caregiver.

Annual retreats meet a different need. One leader spoke of going away on retreat without her family. Like other pastoral leaders who are women, she spoke of the challenge of balancing ministry with parenthood, feeling the burden of maintaining the household and caring for family in addition to overseeing the flock. Wanting an opportunity to experience retreat without maternal responsibilities, this leader started to plan an annual island retreat that was a three-hour drive and ferry ride away. The opportunity to be alone was restorative because she had the opportunity to sleep, engage in artistic outlets, and enjoy time to simply be. Even her family has come to appreciate this time when "mom goes off and does this thing and comes back really calm." She recognized that she was also modeling an important lesson for her family by taking time apart, putting action to the conviction that self-care and retreat are vital components of life and leadership.

So What?

In my first career, I led software engineer teams in developing complex systems and processes. One challenge for software engineers is the desire to advance to the coding stage. The profession has a dangerous misperception that if you are not writing software, then you are not being productive. To reinforce the stereotype, we even had a gauge—productivity measured in lines of code generated.

Pastoral ministry does not have the same kinds of tangible measures, but we work as though it does. As one leader said to me, "Intellectually, I know that if I took an hour every morning to meditate or journal, it would pay for itself spiritually, but I don't.

It's a struggle for me to do." Somehow we feel we must work in a driven and endless manner, as though we will earn a gold star for our efforts.

Accept the invitation to retreat, in little and larger ways. Take 10 minutes of each hour, or one hour each day, or several hours each week, or a week or more each year, and the return on that time of retreat will yield significant dividends. You will be more productive, rested, ready, and able to meet challenges. You will discover the distance needed to identify the objects and answers that remained obscure or illusive when you had your nose to the grindstone. Leaders become more spiritually, emotionally, and physically grounded when we take the time to retreat. Effective leaders take time apart and retreat.

Questions to Consider

1. What are your practices of daily, weekly, and annual retreat?
2. What makes retreat productive for you? Do you need to get away? Do you have a space to retreat in your home? What activities provide retreat for you?
3. With whom in the Bible do you identify when you consider the practice of retreat? What comes to mind when you reflect on their retreat practice?
4. What ideas for retreat arose as you read this chapter?

·5·

release

Cast all of your anxiety on him, because he cares for you.
(1 Peter 5:7)

CONSIDER THE CAMEL. The camel is fitted for the rough desert terrain with padded feet, a muscular body, and a hump of fat able to sustain the camel's life on long journeys. A young camel is able to walk for 100 miles, without rest, food, or water. He is able to carry as much as 1,000 pounds on his back. The camel is a true beast of burden: an animal suited to handle a heavy load and travel great distances.

In this regard pastors function like camels. We carry the concerns of our congregants like a heavily laden camel. We load them on our backs and walk with them for miles. I remember many occasions when I woke in the middle of the night to find myself praying the roster of my membership in alphabetical order. It was a constant practice of my pastoral care, one common to many pastors. It is a practice we do not turn off; we cannot turn it off. We hear prayer needs, take on the concerns, and shoulder them in our spirits. Those pastoral concerns become a collection of cares and burdens that pile up and weigh us down.

But human beings are not camels, and the time comes when we must release the load. Scripture's word of encouragement in 1 Peter 5:7 is fitting, especially when pastors compare ourselves to a camel. When a camel is unloaded, the animal is encouraged to kneel down. Then the camel is urged to roll or lean sideways to cast off or discharge the load. This action is consistent with the image Peter provides for us: "Cast all your cares on him [Christ], because he cares for you."

Even though pastoral leaders are willing to carry the burdens of those for whom we care, we are encouraged by God to kneel, roll to one side, and unload. It is then that we shift the burdens from our backs and roll them onto the Lord. God wants to carry our load. God wants to carry our burdens. Cast your cares on the Lord for he cares about you. This is the invitation to release.

The Need for Release

Each of us has a need for release. We need to let go of challenges and concerns in the midst of our busyness. A colleague of mine and I had the privilege of working with a group of leaders who sought to better integrate spiritual practices into their leadership. As we gathered for one of our face-to-face interactions, I could not help but notice and feel a certain level of anxiety in those initial moments. A palpable tension manifested itself as we came together.

Some of the leaders had to drive for hours to reach the retreat center on time. Some had to catch planes and worried about finding transportation from a busy airport to the sleepy, remote location. They came from their homes with concerns about who would manage family matters while they were gone. They came from offices concerned about whether they had sent that one last e-mail, submitted a necessary report, or left appropriate instructions for others to follow in their absence. The pastors among the group were wondering about what would happen in their congregations while they were gone. What was the plan in case of a church emergency? Had they communicated clearly to staff members or lay leaders regarding the proper procedures and protocols if a need arose?

Based on these myriad concerns, I watched leaders and became caught up myself in the angst of our gathering. The leaders dragged suitcases behind them and clutched cell phones in their hands. They had arrived physically, but they were mentally absent, still distracted by and anxious about last-minute phone calls and final e-mails. Their focus was on tying up various loose ends, hoping these acts would allow them being present for the three-day gathering.

They had accepted the invitation for retreat. But they had not yet achieved release. Ministry and family cares and concerns continued to consume their minds and spirits. That experience made clear to me that people need an opportunity to unwind and release. While leaders may boast of an ability to multitask, switching gears and contexts takes time.

Years ago, I wrote software for a new operating system. The code traversed the stacks of the system to accomplish a function or perform a calculation, but as any software developer could tell you, the process took time. As the programmer, I had to wind my way down, systematically traversing the levels of the code. The same was true to exit the microcode. I had to unwind the procedure to come out of the stack. It was a key lesson of software development at that time.

We must go through the same unwinding process as human beings. We need to slow down and get off the mental roller coaster racing through our minds. We need to sort through our concerns and let go of each one so our minds can be present with our bodies. We need to release, slowly and systematically working our way through the stacks of cares.

My experience in observing busy leaders struggle to transition from one demand to another is just one example of a need for release. Release is required any time we switch contexts and move from one demand to another. As pastors seeking sanctuary, that release is all the more critical because we often resist putting down the mantle of our pastoral roles. We are reluctant to let go. We may switch contexts, but we continue to function in our pastoral role. Even in retreat, leaders are too often susceptible to overfunctioning.

I remember once canvassing a neighborhood to conduct a community survey. I wasn't representing the church or acting as a faith leader in the community. I was just being an involved citizen—at first. But stopping at one home on my list, I met a lovely elderly woman who was delighted to talk. I learned she had just gotten out of the hospital after several days, and in that moment the community canvasser disappeared. Hearing about her physical ailment, without thinking, I was on duty as pastor. I felt compelled to serve.

Introducing myself as a pastor, I asked, "May I pray for you?" When she eagerly agreed, I put down my clipboard, called my canvassing partner over to join hands, and we prayed.

Later that day as we returned to our homes, my partner shared the details of the incident with other volunteers who had come with us. My fellow canvassers marveled over what had happened, but I saw my actions as part of what I do as a minister. It is part of my call. I cannot help but serve when the need arises. I jokingly call it a pastor's occupational hazard, and I am not the only one who will embrace it. This is a good thing. We are called to serve without hesitation and offer care in response to a need.

But I also recognize leaders cannot always be "on." Sometimes we have to turn off those tendencies so that we can rest. We have to set aside those tendencies to receive ministry on occasion. This is what God wants for us. At times, the caretaker must be open to times in which he or she receives care from others. The caretaker needs opportunities to stop and release, casting every care on the Lord. Because God cares for us, God wants to relieve us of our burdens and nurture us. We need release.

What Is Release?

Release is an invitation to slow down. We are always in such a hurry, rushing to and fro. Release encourages us to decelerate and observe ourselves because too often, we do not even recognize we are in a hurry.

Years ago while on vacation in Jamaica, I was walking the beach. I did not give thought to the pace at which I walked. I simply walked at my normal rate of speed, which to be honest is a pretty healthy clip. Suddenly, a woman ran up and grabbed my arm. She said, "What's wrong? Why are you walking so fast?" From her perspective I was virtually running, and the only reason to walk at such a rapid pace was because of an emergency. Why else would someone practically sprint across the beach in beautiful Jamaica?

In hindsight, I am touched by the woman's concern for me. It never occurred to me that I was rushing. Obviously I was, and I needed a complete stranger to help me slow down and recognize what surrounded me. I needed to slow down to enjoy the pace and the place, and to realize clarity of my mind and spirit. Only in slowing down can we separate ourselves from the cares we bear while we are hurrying through life and ministry.

Release is an invitation to engage in a period of dormancy. It is an invitation to be more and do less. When was the last time you did absolutely nothing? If you cannot remember such a time, you are not alone. Most of us are constantly busy. In fact, many of us cannot stand the thought of not being busy.

In our churches, we find dozens of things to do. There are people to call or visit, meetings for which to prepare, sermons to write, Scriptures to exegete, and lessons to develop. As a pastor, I never simply sat in my office at the church. If I had nothing on my calendar or to-do list, I found something to occupy my time. If you are anything like me, you spend hours at the church constantly busy and engaged.

However, it is no different when we go home. Women clergy particularly lament feeling as much responsibility in caring for the household as for the church. Domestic chores loom large: dishes to wash, bills to pay, laundry to fold and put away. There are family matters too: spending time with a spouse or tending to children. We will not simply sit. We feel the need to be busy.

Yet, we cannot always be busy. It is an unhealthy existence. We need times of dormancy, times to not do and to cease ministry functions. If we just sit, we may find, in the midst of doing nothing, we can experience renewal and restoration. Dormancy is a part of the natural life cycle, witnessed in animals that hibernate, fields that lie fallow, trees that stand bare through the winter, and bodies that crave sleep.

We have periods of time when we are on, busy, and by our standards, productive. However, there is productivity in rest as well. In dormancy we renew our strength and become refreshed. In dormancy we regain vitality. When we are dormant, we have the opportunity to truly observe our surroundings and regain a sense of focus regarding what is important. Then we can realize a sense of direction. A period of dormancy is productive because it allows us to return to our physical and mental activities with greater energy.

In fact, this is the paradox of dormancy. We do not appreciate the need to be dormant, believing we have an obligation as leaders to be busy. Yet always being on yields diminishing returns. Over time we have less to give. As a result, our output and ability to do for others are diminished.

However, if we take time for release—to accept the invitation to cast our cares on the Lord—we regain strength. In release we muster our resources and restore our reserves. By doing nothing, we are prepared to do more when the time comes to reengage.

Scriptural Grounding for Release

When Peter said "cast all your anxieties on him, because he cares for you," he was alluding to Psalm 55:22, which reads: "Cast your burden on the LORD, and he will sustain you; he will never permit the righteous to be moved." Specifically in casting off, we are encouraged to unload and release what we have taken upon ourselves. Our confidence in God comes from the knowledge that we can release our burdens and our cares to the Lord. We can literally give it all over to God.

We can stop: stop functioning, stop doing, and stop performing. We can drop: kneel down and prepare to let go. And like the burdened camel, we can roll: that is, release our cares and burdens and everything we have been carrying. God wants us to shift and release the load. God, our sustainer, will carry the load out of loving concern for us.

It is interesting to note the word *burden* in Psalm 55:22 means "what has been given to us [by providence]." Implicit in that meaning is the idea that our burden is a gift. This is not the typical connotation of the English word. When we think of a burden, we think of something heavy or taxing. However, to consider a burden as a gift is fitting when we reflect on the pastoral ministry.

The unction and motivation to serve are part of the divine calling on our lives. We want to extend ourselves to others because our call compels us to do so. Therefore, when we awaken in the middle of the night to pray or are summoned to meet with congregants in situations of pastoral care, we consider it part of what we are called to carry. We acknowledge a sense of providence because we have been entrusted with the care of God's people.

This sense of providence does not negate the reality that the load gets heavy at times and we are not able to carry it all or carry it alone. In fact, this is the challenge of pastoral ministry. Entrusted with the confidences and concerns of a congregation, the pastor is sometimes overwhelmed. Unable to unburden, leaders struggle to carry the load, functioning too often in isolation. In such cases, what is a gift becomes a source of anxiety and worry. As Proverbs 12:25 observes, "Anxiety weighs down the human heart, but a good word cheers it up."

In the Gospels, Jesus admonished the crowds about worry. In Matthew 6:27 and in Luke 12:25, Jesus asked who can add a single hour to life by worrying. Because we cannot affect the smallest of circumstances by worrying, Jesus encouraged the people not to worry at all. He effectively urges us to submit, release, and let go of our cares and concerns.

We cannot change our circumstances by being anxious; therefore, we should release our anxieties. We are to consider the birds of the air and the flowers in the fields. God is mindful of every creature, which is why the Lord provides for them. And as Jesus emphasized in Matthew 10:31, we are so much more valuable than the birds. In Luke 12:7, Jesus tells us God even knows the number of hairs on our head. That is the depth of God's concern for us. It is a concern so great that God knows us far more intimately than we know ourselves.

In recognizing that deep level of divine concern, we can give ourselves over to release. When we let go of our cares and anxieties, God is able to demonstrate constant care and provision by helping us to shoulder the load. This is why Paul says in Philippians 4:6, "Do not worry about anything, but in everything by prayer and supplication with thanksgiving let your requests be made known unto God." Instead of worrying, release everything to God. As Philippians 4:7 affirms, in exchange for our worries and burdens, God gives us peace that surpasses understanding, guards our hearts, and protects us from further worry or concern.

It is worth noting the subtle shift in the language between the words of the psalmist, who encouraged us to cast our cares (our providential gift) on the Lord, and the encouragement of Peter. The apostle exhorted the early Christians to cast their anxiety on the Lord. The implication in Peter's word choice is that we need to cast off those things that worry and distract us. Our worries cause us to focus on things we cannot control or change. Our worries do not add in a positive way because they unnecessarily wear us down.

Instead, we can remember and be encouraged by the words Moses said to Joshua in Deuteronomy 31:8, "God is striding ahead of you. He's right there with you. He won't let you down; he won't leave you. Don't be intimidated. Don't worry" (MSG). We can release the things that concern us to the Lord. God cares enough to carry our anxieties as well as our ministry cares.

Taken together, the Scriptures encourage us to release everything—the good and the bad—to the Lord. God cares for us too much to want us burdened in any way, not by our providential lot or by our anxious worries. Instead, we can rely completely and fully on the Lord, trusting in the depth of the measure of our Creator's concern for us.

What Pastoral Leaders Say about Release

As leaders described their spiritual practices in taking time apart from their leadership context, I recognized a common thread in terms of a need to release. Release was the practice that allowed pastoral leaders to let go of current challenges and slow down to move through and prepare for the next task.

For example, one pastor spoke of a need to engage in periods of silence in the midst of his busyness. In the silence this leader was able to relax, breathe deeply, and prepare for the work ahead. The silence allowed him to release his cares, put them in perspective, and realize a sense of "at-one-ment." He was at one with himself, with his surroundings, and with the challenges that confronted him. As a result, he found himself more compassionate in dealing with others, even in times of challenge. Moreover, through this practice of release, he was able to experience himself as more alive and attuned.

Another pastor also commended silence as part of her practice of release. She noted, "Often prayer is speaking to God, but the silence is both speaking and listening to God and that is profound." She recalled a silent retreat during which she participated in the 30-day Ignatian spiritual exercises. After ten days of silence, her cohort had a break during which talking was permitted. Similarly, after the twentieth day, there was a break as well. She said, "I could hardly wait for the tenth day at the beginning, and I could hardly imagine going back into speaking at the end." She came to recognize how much noise and busyness crowd the course of our daily lives. In silence as she listened for and heard from God, she experienced a tremendous sense of power.

Hearkening back to her Methodist roots, she shared that the release gained in silence was a reminder of the prevenient grace of God—the grace that precedes one's decision to respond to the reconciling invitation of God given through Jesus Christ. Having had that opportunity to release by engaging in silence, she was reminded of God's love for her and could appreciate how God had extended grace to her first.

Another leader exercised dormancy as his practice of release. He spent time alone, just praying, reading, or doing nothing at all. Afterward, this pastor felt emboldened and reaffirmed in who he was and who he had been called to be. By being dormant, this leader learned to be more patient. Release through dormancy enabled him to more creative and to make wiser choices. Moreover, it allowed him to experience a more authentic space, which made him more comfortable with the work and challenges of leadership.

After having to layoff a number of people from the faith-based organization she led, one leader of a faith-based organization acquiesced to a practice of release when she faced the need to layoff forty people only days before Christmas. Taking responsibility for terminating dozens of loyal employees during the holidays was just one aspect of the leadership challenge. She knew there would also be significant trauma for those who remained in the organization as they wrestled with survivor's guilt and the uncertain future of a struggling organization. Her legal counsel told her not to get emotional, but just anticipating the experience was so devastating she had to release.

Huge challenges such as these cannot be taken lightly, nor can they be rushed. This leader knew she needed time to disengage and be dormant. She said, "I spent a good amount of time sitting in low or no light, thinking in my living room—just thinking and praying and reflecting on my role as a leader." And during that time, she prepared for what she needed to do. Reflecting upon these memories this leader said, "I took a lot of time just being still and quiet and girding myself for those meetings with people who were losing their jobs and the staff that was remaining."

Finally, there is my story regarding the practice of release, which I used to reconnect with God. I attended a pastors retreat where a retreat leader spoke of how ministers have inadequate prayer lives—how we don't spend nearly enough time connected to God. He challenged us to spend one hour a day in prayer. One hour a day. But he didn't just challenge us; he gave us the space to do it.

Our instruction was to take five minutes to find a quiet space. We were not to return to our rooms. We could not take our phones. The speaker gave us a single sheet of paper with a translated version of the Twenty-third Psalm and told us to sit, listen, meditate on the psalm, and wait to hear what God would say to us. He said, if our minds wandered that was all right. We were allowed to take a pen and encouraged to write down whatever stray thoughts crossed our minds—a practice of release—and then return to meditation and listening. He said, "Write. . . . Whatever God says to you, write it down."

I found a space in an open field and sat on an old tree stump next to a used fire pit. I looked out over a grove of pine trees, felt the breeze on my face, and closed my eyes. I sat in silence for a moment and simply relished the time. No phone. No thoughts of work—at least for the moment. Having been invited to encounter God, I began to meditate on these words:

> When the Lord is my shepherd, I lack nothing! He is able, even in dry inhospitable desert terrain with a multitude of circling confusing paths, to lead me to the right path that brings me to the rare grassy patches and by restful waters, where I can lie down completely satiated.[1]

As I meditated on the words, I found myself settling in as if I had been covered by a warm blanket. I found myself leaning back as though I had just crawled into my Daddy's lap. I heard the voice of God say, "Rest" and "Lay down." As I continued to listen, God called me "Daughter," and said I was "Home." I felt tears begin to run down my face as the Lord said, "Mine," "Lean on me," and that I was "Anointed."

As I heard these words and wrote them down, I found myself questioning and asking, "Is it you?" I immediately heard God say, "Be certain." The Spirit told me to "persevere," and even chastised me when I failed to write the word down. Finally, I heard God say, "My leader, lead my people."

This was an encounter of release. I had retreated, taking time apart from the normal routines and confines of my leadership context. That was an important first step. But even though I was physically away from the office, I had not yet let go of my cares and anxieties. I was still mentally carrying my responsibilities. I needed to simply be. That is, I had to sit in an open field, allow myself to do nothing, and engage in dormancy.

When I did release, I was able to meditate on God's Word. This enabled me to hear from the Lord, to encounter God's love, and to feel refreshed in the Spirit's presence. Truly God is still speaking. We just have to let go long enough to hear the Lord.

Why Do We Need Release?

Often leaders have the responsibility of being up front, keeping the energy going. We orchestrate because we see this as a core aspect of leadership. Because this is our tendency as leaders, at times we overfunction and continue to process details even when our bodies are physically at rest. One leader characterized this as a "hamster-wheel brain"—the image of a brain in perpetual motion, always thinking, always considering, always multitasking.

Many of us attribute our success to having a hamster-wheel brain. We deal rapidly with a number of issues and simultaneously manage a number of tasks. We are always planning the next visit, sermon, class, or initiative. Yet, there is a downside. The constant motion implied by a hamster-wheel brain can create stress, anxiety, and tension, even when there was no need for such concerns. A strategy is necessary to help leaders let go of anxiety-generating tendencies. This is the purpose of release. Pastoral leadership requires decompression time when we can slow down physically, mentally, and emotionally.

As children, my sister and I used to play with my mother's old stereo from college. The stereo was so old it supported vinyl records that could be played at speeds of 16, 33, 45, and 78 rpm. One of our favorite pastimes was to play records at differing speeds. At 78 rpm, our favorite singers sounded like chipmunks. At 16 or 33 rpm, the voices were in slow motion. I cannot help but relate that slow-motion sound to the practice of release. Like a song playing at a speed too slow for the intended recording, we need to just...go...slow.

Most of us operate like a record at 78 rpm. We madly run about not recognizing we are operating at a heightened state and pace. Our heart rates are elevated, our breathing becomes shallow, and our blood pressure may increase. However, by slowing down and engaging in release, we settle to a more normal speed. Our heart rate slows and breathing deepens. Pent-up anxieties have an opportunity to fall away or at least be placed on hold momentarily. In exchange for stress, we regain a sense of calmness.

This is why we engage in release. As one leader noted, the downtime offers "the space to release myself from things beyond my control." It is an invitation to disengage from the challenges of the day. Moreover, through release we are able to refuel, to ready ourselves for what comes next. It supplies the opportunity to slow the hamster-wheel brain to reduce stress that causes tension and anxiety. Through release, whether it takes the form of silence, prayer, or inactivity, we transition from one task to the next, prepared and restored with the energy necessary to lead.

What Can You Do to Release?

In some regards release should be one of the easiest practices in which to engage. However, it proves to be one of the most difficult things for pastoral leaders to do. Begin with simple and familiar practices. You may be drawn to a time of silent meditation, using a favorite passage of Scripture. You may find that having an hour to sit and meditate on Psalm 23 or a similar text is a gift. And while your mind may wander at first, write down those wanderings. That simple act should allow you to let go of those stray thoughts as well.

Just as Elijah discovered, you will find God in the silence as a still, small voice. In the silence God speaks, and as we focus on hearing that divine voice and on being in the Spirit's presence, we have the chance to give those challenges and burdens to God. When we cast our cares on the Lord, we receive the peace of God that surpasses all understanding in exchange.

There are other ways in which to engage in release. Take a moment right now to close your eyes and breathe deeply. Deep breathing has the ability to slow our heart rates and blood pressure. Spending a few minutes each hour to intentionally breathe in and out provides the capacity to let go and lean into the blessing of doing nothing. In fact, that is what is encouraged in release. We are encouraged to do whatever will allow us to disconnect.

For some, release is realized in stillness. As Psalm 46:10 says, "Be still and know that I am God!" What are ways you can be still? Some leaders reacquaint themselves with the joys of taking a nap. Sometimes a rest in the middle of the day is the perfect release from confronting challenges.

Alternatively, you might opt to sit and just enjoy some down time. I remember having the opportunity to sit in my dining room early in the morning. I watched the rising sun's reflection on the walls. In that moment I realized I had never seen the light on the walls. I had never sat still long enough to see it. We need the down time—that opportunity to simply sit and rest in the moment. It is the down time that makes it possible for us to go on.

Others might desire to combine the practice of release with movement. Disciplines such as yoga and tai chi, which involve physical, mental, and spiritual practices to attain peace and well-being, both offer deep breathing and meditation through stretching, positioning, and patterned movement. Walking is part of my personal practice of release. Being guilty of sitting at my computer for hours at a stretch, I sometimes feel tension begin to build. In those moments, I take a break and go for a walk. The break is the practice of retreat, but during my walk, I practice release. I use the time to listen to music, talk to God, or sing aloud as I go. With each step, I feel tension and stress drain away, and I experience peace in the process.

Some pastors make it a point to go to the gym for a workout as their means of release. The opportunity to expend energy allows them to relieve stress. One leader feels like he can do anything after going to the gym! Having the opportunity to work out energizes and empowers him to handle anything that comes his way.

So What?

The experience of release is like having a heavy pack removed from our backs. We are lighter, freer, and often feel we can do anything because we have taken the opportunity to just let go for a few minutes. Release is like a contented sigh; we regain a sense of peace and tranquility. Unburdened, we feel at ease. It is like being led to still waters and green pastures where we can lie down.

Beyond that unburdening, release prepares us for the next task of our day. Release allows us to clear space mentally and emotionally so we can ready ourselves to address whatever comes. Release refuels and restores us, making it possible to return to work more meaningfully engaged.

When I spoke to one leader about her practice of release, she described getting into her car to drive to her favorite retreat location. As she shared, she sighed, closing her eyes and speaking of the calm she felt, with significant emphasis on the vowel sound of the word calm. In her very words, she was expressing release and saw it as a gift to lay down her concerns.

An old gospel hymn encourages us to take our burdens to the Lord and leave them there. Release is that invitation. We can release our cares to the Lord, because God cares for us.

Questions to Consider

1. What are your practices of release? What do you do to let go of the challenges that confront you in leadership?

2. Do you feel guilty when you do nothing (which is essential to the practice of release)? If so, what might you do to overcome that feeling of guilt, so you can create and protect time for release in your life?

3. During release we are encouraged to cast our cares on the Lord, giving up our worries for the peace of God that surpasses understanding. Remember a time when you gave up your worries and experienced a sense of peace. What was happening for you in that moment?

4. What ideas for release arose as you read this chapter?

NOTE

1. John Piippo, pastors retreat handout, April 22, 2013.

·6·

review

God made my life complete when I placed all the pieces before him. When I got my act together, he gave me a fresh start. Now I'm alert to GOD's ways; I don't take God for granted. Every day I review the ways he works; I try not to miss a trick. I feel put back together, and I'm watching my step. God rewrote the text of my life when I opened the book of my heart to his eyes. (Psalm 18:20-24, The Message)

THE SUPERSCRIPT OF Psalm 18 attributes this song to David, in which he praises God for saving him from his enemies. Specifically in verses 20-24, David attributes his deliverance to his faith in God. As he committed himself and his life to God—placing himself before God—David felt he had been given a new start. Moreover, having recognized the move of God in response to his obedience, David became cognizant of a process.

By keeping God's commands in focus and by committing himself to God, David found God ordered his steps. David had had the experience of venturing forth and finding himself in harm's way because of his own desires. Yet, he also knew the deliverance that came from being obedient to God and following God's plan. Following God's plan had far better outcomes than going it alone.

That is why, according to this psalm, David kept himself mindful of God's ways every day. He paid close attention.

Through paying close attention, David recognized two important outcomes. First, David found himself regulated and measured. Through his own devices, David recognized his fallibility. Like all of us, David was prone to fail went he went out on his own. But by following God, David was able to practice restraint because God interposed on his behalf. Thus, David's path became assured and his steps were made firm.

Second, David experienced what felt like a rewriting of his life story. He experienced recompense, being rewarded by God as though he were righteous. David did not see himself as righteous; rather he recognized God's intercession on his behalf. This, to David, was testament to the fact that God knew his heart. In response God made David's path certain as he followed the Lord's plan for his life.

For David, this was a process. It was a process of review. David reviewed the parts and pieces of his life, and in the review David recognized that he experienced a fresh start as he willingly gave his life over to God. The same is true for us. We need to give the parts and pieces of our lives intentionally to God for the Lord's ordering and prioritization. Oftentimes, however, we are not cognizant of all of those pieces without engaging in review. By engaging in review, we submit ourselves to God's way, rather than our own.

A friend of mine is fond of saying God always has a plan B. I would argue that God does not have plan B; rather God has a plan. The issue is that we, in wanting to exert our will and desire, press for our agenda. Too often our agenda becomes a detour, adding additional steps and superfluous activities to our path. Ultimately and ideally, we reach God's intent, but we are mistaken if we believe the circuitous route was God's plan. It is the difference between God's permissive will—wherein God gives us the autonomy and leeway to do it our way—and God's perfect will.

Plan A is God's perfect will. What we experience as plan B is navigated through God's permissive will. The process of review can help us discern the path we are to take. Reviewing what is ours to do and offering it up to God helps us to find order and regulate ourselves in the work we are called to do.

The Need for Review

Why do we need to engage in review? We need review because without it, the tasks of ministry control and consume us. Richard P. DeShon and Abigail Quinn of Michigan State University conducted a study to demonstrate this fact. Their study sought to determine the specific tasks critical to the role of the pastor and the competencies that contributed to job success and effective performance.[1] Their study identified thirteen task clusters of work:

+ Administration
+ Care-giving
+ Communication
+ Connectional services (with denomination or judicatory)
+ Evangelism
+ Facilities management
+ Fellowship
+ Management (of members, leaders, and staff)
+ Preaching and public worship
+ Relationship building
+ Rituals and sacraments (or ordinances)
+ Self-development
+ Spiritual development (of others)

The challenge in ministry is that all of these skills and abilities are needed, complete with the dexterity to use them as the situation demands. That seemed to be one of the surprising results of the study for the researchers. When asked about the work involved in pastoral ministry, clergy cite a diversity of tasks to which they must attend. Yet, when asked, pastors are hard pressed to provide a differentiating rank in the importance of these tasks. Instead, they determine the importance of each task based on current context.

For example, pastors acknowledge that preparing a weekly sermon is important, but when a parishioner is undergoing surgery, making a hospital visit becomes higher priority even though the need to prepare the sermon remains. Each task is essential, even when accomplishing both means doing one or the other in personal time previously set aside for self-care.

I recall a time in my own ministry when the town in which I served experienced a high rate of teen suicide. This emergency situation preempted all other ministry efforts and required a great deal of my time in community involvement and counseling. In this instance, the needs of the community needed to be encompassed alongside the important work of caring for a congregation. Even so, the needs of the congregation did not abate.

These examples illustrate ministry's potential to be all-consuming, which concurs with the findings of the study: that a pastor's work activities are "highly varied, taxing, fast-paced, unrelenting and often fragmented."[2] The nature of such pressing, important, and often unanticipated demands makes pastoral ministry unique and challenging.

Not only does ministry feature a wide diversity of tasks, but ministers need to quickly switch tasks as the need demands. As researchers remarked, "The breadth of tasks performed by local church pastors coupled with the rapid switching between task clusters and roles that appears prevalent in this position is unique. I have never encountered such a fast-paced job with such varied and impactful responsibilities."[3]

How does a pastoral leader keep track of what needs to be done and provide the appropriate prioritization of responsibilities within ministry? This is the challenge. Because some tasks loom large each week if not attended to, it is too easy to succumb to doing what is right in front of us, seeing those tasks as most pressing. However, pastoral ministry through this approach becomes ineffective as our work becomes tactical engagement without strategic direction.

Review is the essential response to this leadership challenge. We need to be able to review the work we are to do. We need to be able to lay out the parts and pieces in an intentional way as we seek God's wisdom to help us prioritize and organize. Without intentional review, we risk being disjointed and scattered in our efforts.

We rush from one demand to another, feeling tossed and pulled. We may focus on minor tasks while ignoring major ones. Review helps us to consider the work in a mindful way to determine how the parts and pieces go together, to examine our prioritizations, and then to move faithfully forward having discerned the way to go. Through review, we feel more ordered and established, knowing the work in which we engage is the right work and the right task at the right time.

What Is Review?

Review invites leaders to consider their ministry context mindfully, without personal condemnation. There are two concepts of importance in this definition. First, there is the idea of mindful review of the work. Mindfulness speaks of intentionality. Review is a process of intentionally considering a task or effort in order to truly experience that effort in full.

I once led a seminar in which I had participants mindfully eat a raisin. After distributing a couple of raisins to each participant, we took a minute simply to look at the raisin and examine its contours. Next, I told them to put a single raisin in their mouths, but they were not allowed to bite down. They were to solely experience the feel of the raisin on their tongue. After a minute, I allowed people to take one bite, just piercing the raisin with their teeth. I urged them to experience the taste of the ruptured raisin, the sweetness that poured forth and how the taste differed from the experience of the unbitten raisin moments before. When I finally allowed them to chew the raisin, I asked participants to make the raisin last as long as possible, chewing slowly and intentionally until nothing was left in their mouths.

It was an amazing experience. Some participants spoke about how much they salivated while just holding a raisin. Their mouths watered in anticipation of a sensation that was delayed in coming. Others noted how the experience caused them to recognize they had never fully tasted a raisin before because they had never taken the time to savor its flavor. Some said it had never occurred to them to take so much time to eat anything and how the sensation of eating was heightened because of the experience. A raisin is one of those things we simply pop into our mouths without much thought, easily consuming a snack-sized package within a minute or two. However, as we are mindful about our eating, we open ourselves to a new awareness and are able to truly taste and experience in full.

A second aspect of review is to consider our current context *without condemnation*. This is a big challenge. When was the last time you really sat down to review the yet-to-be-done work on your task list? More often than not, in review we will remember a task important to us that has slipped our minds.

How do you react when you remember some responsibility, task, or effort you have forgotten to address? Most of us are incredibly hard on ourselves. One pastor shared how she had forgotten a friend was undergoing surgery. She had promised to come to the hospital early in the morning to pray with the family prior to surgery, but the promise had slipped her mind. As she sat at her breakfast table with coffee in hand, she opened her email only to realize she was two hours late for the scheduled surgery. In that moment, her stomach dropped and tears threatened to fall. How could she have forgotten? How could she have been so careless?

Immediately she switched gears, rushing to her car and racing to get to the hospital. When she arrived, the wife of the patient was sitting in the waiting area with an expression of pure joy to see this pastor friend. She was so happy to have the company of this pastor to pass the time while she waited for the surgery to complete. The pastor, however, was still berating herself for failing to arrive at the hospital when promised.

This is the challenge of reviewing our ministry context without condemnation. We are bound to remember tasks in our review that we meant to do or should have done. It will be tempting to abandon the process of review to jump up and rush headlong into the forgotten task. I encourage you to put that temptation aside—at least for the moment. We need to engage in review with a mindset that calmly considers the parts and pieces, watching them float by as freely as the clouds in the sky.

As we review mindfully what we have to do, without condemning ourselves for what we may have forgotten, we can better recognize and become aware of the full scope of our work—both the strategic aspects as well as the tactical. By reviewing these tasks and offering them intentionally to God, we ask the Spirit for priority and leading so we are better able to discern the necessary direction for the work of our calling.

Scriptural Grounding for Review

The Bible does not often use a word that we translate as *review*. However, consider where the idea of review is used. *The Message* uses the English word *review* three times: 1 Samuel 12:7; 2 Samuel 22:23; and Psalm 18:22. The latter two references quote David's words, "Every day I review the ways [God] works, I try not to miss a trick." In this use, review is a process of mental reconsideration. David is remembering and reconsidering God's ways in his life.

In 1 Samuel 12:7, Samuel recalled God's faithful righteousness toward Israel, even as Israel demonstrated disobedience toward God. Samuel said, "Take your stand before him now as I review your case before GOD in the light of all the righteous ways in which GOD has worked with you and your ancestors." Samuel remembered and then identified for the Israelites the many instances in which the Lord responded faithfully toward the people. In sharing these examples, Samuel engaged the process of review. In this case, Samuel was calling to remembrance God's graciousness to his people.

This use of the word is in keeping with what I am naming the process of review. It is the act of calling to mind and articulating what is remembered in a way that allows us to identify distinctive acts or activities. Such identification provides for an ordering that makes the case and establishes the argument. Samuel was effectively saying, "I have reviewed the work of God and God has been faithful in every case."

The New Revised Standard Version of the Bible uses a synonym of the word review, which is assess. Leviticus 27 speaks of votive offerings to the Lord where the priests determine an acceptable offering. In each verse where the word assess is used, the work of the priest is to examine the case of the individual, review the circumstances, and decide what is most appropriate. For example, Leviticus 27:12 reads: "The priest shall assess it: whether good or bad, according to the assessment of the priest, so it shall be." While there is a financial aspect in the usage, assess also encompasses the idea of reviewing a decision to make a determination.

The Message uses the word assess in a similar way in Numbers 13:17-20. When Moses sent out the spies from the tribes of Israel to scout the Promised Land, he encouraged them to "assess the people" of Canaan to determine whether they were strong or weak. They needed to make a judgment call based on what they saw, and in making that judgment, they engaged in the process of review.

In the *Living Bible*, Ecclesiastes 8:1 declares, "How wonderful to be wise, to understand things, to be able to analyze them and interpret them. Wisdom lights up a [person's] face, softening its hardness." This Scripture depicts an excellent example of the process of review. In review, we analyze a situation and interpret the effects to establish a plan. This ability compares to the kind of wisdom illuminated in one's face. This is what review does. Through the process of review, we can sort the complex tasks or pieces, gain a sense of priority, and emerge with peace that comes from such simplification.

The New American Standard Bible uses the word assess in Luke 12:56. There Jesus chastises the crowd for being able to analyze the skies to determine the weather, but being unable to similarly discern the sign of the times. The implication is we can systematically make determinations based on an assessment or review of a situation. In this case, by accurately assessing the weather, we can properly prepare. It involves a process of review. We assess and analyze a situation and are then able to govern ourselves accordingly.

This is what review commends in the Bible and it is what review commends for our effectiveness as leaders. As we review the work before us, seeking God's help for prioritization, we emerge with a sense of direction more ordered and balanced than had we simply operated from our own devices and desires.

What Pastoral Leaders Say about Review

One leader recalled an incredibly stressful time in her career. She spoke of awakening at night with an inability to sleep. In those restless moments, she pulled out a notebook and began writing the things she needed to do the next day. While there was a level of anxiety associated with the process, there was also a sense of unburdening. That process of putting her thoughts down on paper so the tasks did not seem so overwhelming made a difference and enabled this leader to get the sleep she needed.

I operate similarly. In my ministry work, I constantly switch contexts to completely unrelated tasks. In one moment, I am providing pastoral care. Minutes later, I am speaking with a vendor regarding new equipment I am considering purchasing. The tasks are so different the abrupt shifts are sometimes jarring.

The process of review allows my day to have a semblance of order. By writing down the varying tasks and simply sitting with the work that needs to be done, I can better sense where to focus my efforts and attentions. Through the process of review, I perceive the synergies between seemingly unrelated tasks. Through review, I am far less likely to be overwhelmed because I know what must be done now versus what can be delayed. Review enables me to assess where to put my energies so I remain vitalized for the work.

Why Do We Need to Review?

Perhaps you have heard of the Tyranny of the Inbox. It is a phenomenon when we work with an almost mechanistic frenzy, trying futilely to empty our paper, electronic, and mental inboxes of work. There is no real thought or consideration to our efforts. What comes in must go out, and we keep at it as though we can actually catch up.

Sometimes this is a reasonable approach to work. Just as time and motion coaches of decades past spoke of handling a piece of mail only once, efficiency experts today say the same thing for the email that inundates our inboxes. Read the email and dispense it then and there, rather than allowing it to accumulate in the inbox only to have to reread it later when we actually determine how best to dispose of or dispense with the message.

The work of pastoral ministry is not so easily dispensable. First, there are a variety of tasks or efforts to consider, many of which are comprised of complex, dependent, intermediate steps. Second, the tasks are often all high priority. Is it more important to visit the congregant going into surgery, to work on the Sunday sermon, or to provide counseling to a couple whose marriage is in trouble? How do you possibly decide? You cannot do everything, but what is the appropriate priority?

This is why we need review. We need a process through which we can identify all the tasks and competing priorities in order to make a determination about how we will govern ourselves and our time. But review is more than making a list. In this context review is a spiritual process, through which we offer ourselves, along with the parts and pieces of our lives, to God.

Matthew 6:33 tells us, "Strive first for the kingdom of God and his righteousness, and all of these things will be given to you as well." Jesus offered these words to discourage us from worrying, but implied in the verse is a divine ordering applicable to all aspects of our lives. Rather than becoming anxious about the competing, high priority tasks in our lives, we can hand them over to God. When we hand tasks over to God, God will give us a sense of ordering through which we will know what must come first.

I was in my office one evening working on a presentation for an upcoming workshop when I received a call from the granddaughter of a church member. She explained that her grandmother, who had been placed in a nursing home, was failing and would I please go see her right away?

In my mind I wrestled over what to do. I needed to finish preparing the presentation I was to deliver only days later. Moreover, I found myself rationalizing—surely it was not so urgent for me to rush to the nursing home immediately. It was after dark; I wanted to make dinner for my family and ensure my son finished his homework. Yet, I found no relief in my rationalizations. Dogged by the notion that I needed to go, I did. I had a grace-filled visit with my member, and I got home with time to prepare dinner, help my son with his homework, and finish the presentation as the work progressed with amazing speed and efficiency.

The next morning, I received a call informing me that the elderly congregant had died. Shocked by the news, I was also filled with gratitude. In the moment of decision making, I had not named my process "review," but that was exactly the process I employed. In listing all the competing tasks of the moments, I developed a different ordering of what was of the greatest priority. Had I operated of my own volition, I would not have been available to minister to my member, and the guilt of that decision would have had lasting repercussions. But God gave me a new ordering and as I submitted to the Spirit's priorities, all things—ministering to my member in her transition, spending time with my family, and completing my presentation—were added unto me.

What Can You Do to Review?

In the holiday classic *It's a Wonderful Life*, George Bailey's daughter Zuzu won a flower in school that she tried to keep alive in the folds of her coat. As anyone who has ever observed children can imagine, that flower was probably worse for wear smothered in the little girl's coat than it would have been carried in the open. Having been so mishandled, petals began to fall off the flower and in response the little girl was understandably upset. She said to her father, picking at the fallen petals, "Paste it, Daddy, paste it," wanting him to remedy the situation.

Review is like seeing ministry tasks as fallen flower petals and asking God to "paste" them. In other words, we invite God to help us organize the disparate pieces of our work into a coherent whole that helps us be more established and certain regarding the way to go. We offer up the petals and trust God to help us discern between better and best so we can know to what we should say yes, and just as important, to what we should say no.

The crushed flower analogy may help us appreciate that all of what we do or endeavor to do is important. At least, we believe what we are trying to do is important, but we cannot accomplish it all in a single span of time. So, as we offer the petals of our scattered tasks up to God and seek the Lord's wisdom and insight, we gain a sense of where to direct our efforts.

Sit for a moment and get comfortable. Consider the work you have to do. Maybe you need to write a sermon. Perhaps you have committed to address a group or lead a meeting. There is a baby dedication coming up and you need to meet with the parents. Someone is in the hospital and you need to visit. What about time for your personal study and meditation? Plus, you promised your family you would go out to the movies or have a quiet night at home.

Each of these things is important, but what is most important? Take a deep breath and then let it go. See each task as a fragile flower petal. Each is a part of the precious whole. Offer the petals up to God. *Paste it, Daddy. Paste it, Mommy.* As you sit in the silence, what thought or feeling surfaces for you? As you sit in silence, what task are you most drawn to complete? Can you feel the leading of the Holy Spirit? To what are you being directed?

I imagine this is what David was doing in Psalm 18. He was reviewing his life and offering it up to God. We need to make a habit of engaging in this kind of review daily to check in with God and recognize the Lord's priority and plan. What we believe is top priority may not be God's priority. However, we will not recognize that priority unless we review. David said he felt like God was putting him back together and ordering the pieces of his life. That sifting process makes firm our footsteps by helping us see a path rather than an insurmountable obstacle. Review gives us a fresh start because it allows God to put the pieces back together in a way that aligns with the divine purpose for our lives.

So What?

David's characterization of review in Psalm 18 aptly lists the beneficial outcomes of the process. Review gives us a fresh start. Rather than feeling subsumed by the competing, high-priority tasks of pastoral ministry, we can realize a sense of order that offers a fresh start. By gaining a sense of God's divine ordering, we know the progression of the tasks we do first. Life is no longer a jumble of codependent parts and pieces. We start to see a logical progression that makes tasks seem doable. We become alert to God's ways.

I think of my actions in trying to determine whether to visit my member or complete a presentation. Any of the tasks under consideration were good and defensible, but by the grace of God I was able to discern between the good and the better—and I was better for it. As I submitted to God's priority for the tasks I was considering, I became more cognizant of God's active role in my life. In this way, I became like David, able to say, "I try not to miss a trick."

What makes us better is an illuminated pathway. Psalm 37:23 reads: "Stalwart walks in step with GOD; his path blazed by GOD, he's happy" (MSG). We can walk with certainty and assurance because we know the way to go. Moreover, as Proverbs 20:24 says, "All steps are ordered by the LORD; how then can we understand our own ways?" God establishes our steps and makes those steps firm when we follow his ways. This is a source of joy. As the psalmist noted, by coming out of the pit and being established on a secure rock, we experience a new song, which becomes the cause for offering praise to God.

When we engage in review, we also encounter a sense of peace. Having more tasks to accomplish without a clear sense of priority creates tension and stress. One leader experienced insomnia as the result of an overwhelming workload. When there is clarity and order, however, there is calm and peace. This is not to say review will miraculously allow us to accomplish everything on our long to-do lists every time! However, we start to recognize that not everything is urgent—because when everything is urgent, nothing is.

Our ability to see prioritization and order comes from review. When we submit to review, God will rewrite the text of our lives and help us to realize an illumined path and plan for the work we are called to do.

Questions to Consider

1. Take a moment to review the work you have to do. What is happening to you during this process of review? Does it make you anxious because you recognize many competing priorities, or does it produce calmness because you can arrange all ideas in one place? Why?

2. Imagine the tasks you list as clouds floating by in the sky. Does this vision help you relax as you engage in review? If not, what other image may help?

3. Read Exodus 18:13-27. How was Moses' process of hearing the complaints of the children of Israel in the wilderness like the tyranny of the inbox? How did Moses' father-in-law, Jethro, help him with the process of review?

4. Why is it important to engage in review without condemnation?

5. What ideas for review occurred to you as you read this chapter?

NOTES

1. Richard P. DeShon and Abigail Quinn, "Job Analysis Generalizability Study for the Position of United Methodist Local Pastor: Focus Group Results," General Board of Higher Education and Ministry (GBHEM), December 15, 2007.

2. Gary William Kuhne and Joe F. Donaldson, "Balancing Ministry and Management: An Exploratory Study of Pastoral Work Activities," *Review of Religious Research*, Volume 37, No. 2, 1995, 147–63.

3. DeShon and Quinn, 20.

·7·

reconnect

Now the LORD *said to Abram, "Go from your country and your kindred and your father's house to the land that I will show you."*
(Genesis 12:1)

WHEN GOD CALLED Abram, the call was specific. God said leave your country. God said leave your family. God told Abram to go to a land that would be shown to him. Moreover, God told Abram that his name would be great. He would be blessed to be a blessing. He would be a great nation. People who blessed Abram would be blessed, and people who cursed Abram would be cursed. These were the instructions God gave to Abram. So, Abram faithfully went forth, taking his family and possessions. And when Abram arrived at the land of Canaan, God appeared and said to him, "I will give this land to your descendents."

How did Abram feel? The Bible tells us Abram heard the voice of God and was compelled to go. In fact, his compliance and willingness were attributed to Abram as righteousness. We can understand why he went: Abram had divine assurance through a prophetic vision that he had abundant blessing in store, and that all people would be blessed through him. Greater still, God told Abram his descendants would take possession of the land to which he had traveled.

We can only imagine the excitement such a vision provoked, even as it raised more questions. Where was Abram being led? How would he know he had arrived? How would God's promises come to pass? One promise had to have been beyond imagination. The Bible tells us Abram was 75 years old at the time of this encounter, but he was without children. However, God said Abram would have descendants; there would be a lineage and heirs to follow him. We can only imagine how Abram must have felt, but the range of emotions from trepidation to elation must have been incredible.

In reflecting upon Abram's experience, as pastors we realize that we, too, have such experiences. Remember your own call. What was happening for you in that moment?

I remember one of my experiences very well. I had been recently called to serve as youth pastor of a church. Having a few minutes in my schedule one day, I decided to go over to the church, hoping to pick up the key to the building and introduce myself to members of a committee meeting there that afternoon. Having exchanged pleasantries with the committee members, I asked if I could walk around the church by myself. Up to that point, my tours around the church had been accompanied. But on that day, I felt led to walk around the church alone. I remember so clearly rounding the corner from a stairwell and arriving at the entrance to the baptistery. It was at that moment I heard the voice of God say, "Reclaim my church."

What did the call mean? I had no idea. Whose voice was it? I was sure it was the Lord because the voice and the command were so clear. What did God want me to do? I was not fully certain, but I remember being filled with awe. I also felt excited by the possibilities, inspired by the potential, and filled with hope regarding what this meant for my ministry. God had a work for me to do, and was now calling me to do it. I remember feeling elated and ready to go.

What about you? Do you remember where you were when you heard God's call in your life? Did you receive a vision? Did you have a dream? Did you have a deep sense of knowing and a compulsion to go? Did someone speak a prophecy that nudged you before the words were uttered? And when the word came to you, were you excited or were you frightened? Did you hesitate, or did you readily respond in obedience?

At times in ministry we need to remember and reacquaint ourselves with our call. We need to reflect on that call, on what we were called to do, how we felt, and how we responded. We need to reconnect because it is through reconnecting that we are made alive and renewed with what God wants us to do and where God wants us to go.

The Need to Reconnect

Why do we need to reconnect? Think about the day-to-day work of ministry. At times, ministry has a routine. We lead worship and deliver a sermon on Sunday. Monday is typically a day off, followed by Tuesday staff and committee meetings. Wednesday may be the day for Bible study and midweek services, and on Thursdays, many of us prepare our sermons and ensure everything is ready for Sunday worship. On Friday, we may visit individuals who are ill and continue to work on the sermon. We hope for a little downtime on Saturday to spend with family and friends, but often we are still fine tuning the sermon for Sunday morning.

That is an average week in a nutshell. Interspersed with such mundane activities may be pastoral counseling sessions; preparations for baby dedications, weddings, and funerals; meetings with a variety of people; unexpected community or congregational crises; and unplanned interruptions that invariably crop up. Overall, however, there is an ebb and flow to ministry: sometimes busy, sometimes uneventful. Yet, with so many activities, it is easy to fall into a mindless routine. We find ourselves consumed in the day-to-day, where tasks and activities move around in circles rather than toward a purpose with intent and certainty.

The R of reconnecting takes us off the treadmill, giving our actions trajectory. Reconnecting is the act of intentionally remembering our call with wonder and excitement. The knowledge of call gives meaning and purpose to our ministry. As we reconnect, we remember what God called us to do and recognize the specifics of our call instructions. By reconnecting, we realize we are not adrift; God has already provided insights for our ministry in our original call. Reconnecting with our call also provides renewed vision for our ministry. When we reconnect to the vision, we can know whether we are honoring God's call on our lives. Finally, reconnecting helps us know when we have finished our assignment.

One pastor shared about her struggles in her ministry. She came to the congregation with such excitement, but after a number of years, fatigue set in. She initially had such hope and felt called to share her hope and enthusiasm with the congregation. But now she was drained and tired and looking for direction.

Hers is not an unfamiliar story for many pastoral leaders. This pastor could see the signs of congregational decline. Fewer members gathered on Sunday. Those who did gather represented a generation advanced in age. The sanctuary was largely empty and young adults were nonexistent. There were a few children, but the ages were so disparate she found it difficult to generate any momentum for Sunday school and children's ministry.

Nevertheless, the pastor tried to reengage the flagging congregation. Sunday after Sunday, this pastor tried to muster enthusiasm as she preached. In an effort to generate urgency for their uncertain future, she drew people's attention to the stark realities. In hopes of helping people ignite their faith, she made recommendations for new ministries. She attended church meetings and attempted to point out new possibilities to committee members. Being met with resistance from those in attendance, this pastor often left meetings feeling disappointed and drained of energy.

In the midst of these realities, however, this pastor found herself pulled by a new challenge. She had begun to feel called away from the church. She felt God might be moving her toward something else, but she did not know to what. Even so, she was not able to let go. She found herself attempting one more thing or introducing one more initiative.

Why did she have a need to keep trying even as she sensed God pulling her away? In her mind she had failed. She was burdened by a belief that the only possible outcome for this ministry assignment was for the church to have realized renewal. But because there was no burgeoning Sunday worship with a vibrant Sunday school; because there was not renewed effort in mission and the work of the church in the community or the world, her ministry seemed to be a failure. And because she carried the weight of perceived failure, she could not let go. She could not give up, even though it was increasingly clear God had another plan.

When asked about her call, this pastor immediately responded. She said her calling was to bring hope, energy, and enthusiasm to the church. She was very clear about that. When asked whether she felt she had faithfully fulfilled her call in her current context, her response was almost as immediate. "Yes," she said. Maybe her assignment was complete.

In Exodus 3, God gave Moses an assignment. The Lord told Moses to go to Egypt, confront Pharaoh, and tell Pharaoh to let God's people go. In addition, verse 12 records two very specific aspects of that call: lead the people out of Egypt, and assemble them to worship at God's Holy Mountain.

Did Moses complete his assignment? Yes. Do we think of Moses as being successful in his mission? No, usually we lament Moses and perceive he failed in his assignment. Why? Too often, we conflate the exodus event with the larger Book of Exodus, believing Moses' task was to lead the people out of enslavement in Egypt and on into the Promised Land.

This misperception is exacerbated by the incident recorded in Numbers 20 where God commanded Moses to speak to the rock to bring forth water for the people. Instead, out of frustration with the children of Israel, Moses struck a rock not once, but twice. Water came forth, but in his temper, Moses demonstrated he did not trust God to fulfill the promise. Because of this, God did not allow Moses to lead the people into the Promised Land. However, we cannot lose sight of the fact Moses had already completed his original assignment. He brought the people out of Egypt and ushered them to Mount Sinai to worship God. He did exactly what God had called him to do.

I asked this pastor to, again, consider her assignment. When encouraged to reconnect to what God had called her to do, she knew the answer: her call was to bring hope, energy, and encouragement to the congregation. Yet, she needed to reconnect to what her assignment truly meant—and what it did not mean.

As she reconnected with her call, she was able to recognize that she had been faithful to her assignment. She had done exactly what God called her to do. She remembered with joy her calling to preach the word of life and breath, to help stir up a discouraged people. God had not promised her the church would turn around as a result of her efforts. She had added that component as part of her assignment and felt discouraged by her perceived failure.

But when she reconnected she remembered. Moreover, she had an image of herself on her knees, attending to her work, and as she worked, God tapped her on the shoulder and called her to come away. Thus, not only did reconnecting help her remember her call, but it also helped her to realize that she had been released from her assignment. She had been prepared for a new work to which God was calling her. We, too, need to reconnect to remember and be clear about what God has called us to do.

What Is Reconnecting?

The practice of reconnecting is the invitation to remember God's call on your life and relive the experience of that call. You will rediscover emotions that you felt, the purpose to which you believed God called you, and the desire generated as a result of wanting to live out that purpose. It is the opportunity to remember what is core and central to your ministry in order to refocus on God's path and plan. More than remembering, reconnecting is the opportunity to rekindle the flame of dreams lost, to reacquaint yourself with where you were going. Reconnecting is the invitation to rise above the routine to be enlivened once again to the higher ideals to which you aspire.

Recall an early experience when you pursued a ministry assignment to which you felt called. Do you remember being asked a typical interview question, such as, "Why do you want this position?" You probably fielded questions about your goals for the position and what you wanted to achieve. "How will you bring these ideas to fruition?" the interviewers want to know. In response to such questions, you started to dream and make plans. You began to detail strategies for how to begin and how to proceed through the first months. You undergirded your plans with prayer, knowing that as you committed your plans to the Lord they would be established. In your consideration of that opportunity to do ministry, you got excited about the possibilities. You recognized your gifts and began to project how they would make a difference in that ministry setting. In short, you dreamed. To remember those hopes, plans, and dreams is the process of reconnection.

Reconnecting also enables us to set our sights on a vision far beyond where we presently reside. I remember when I was first struggling with my call to ministry. I had a recurring dream that I was preparing to preach. In my dreams the settings were always different: sometimes I was in a sanctuary; other times I was in a large amphitheater. What was constant was I was always making my way to the pulpit or platform from which I was to preach. However, on my way, I was constantly interrupted by someone wanting something from me. Each time, I would stop to respond. Having dealt with the interruption, I moved forward to preach, only to be interrupted again and again and again. My dreams always ended the same way—I would never make it to the pulpit. After repeated interruptions, I would wake up before I ever reached the microphone.

What were those dreams about? I finally realized I was the one creating the interruptions. God was calling me forward, but I kept hesitating. Ultimately I had to surrender myself and my life to the Lord and step into the call God placed on my life. As I reconnect with my dreams, it is clear some aspects have come to fruition. I have had many occasions to preach in a sanctuary. However, I have yet to make it to an amphitheater. Reconnecting with the thought inspires me. God had a plan for my ministry, and the Spirit gave me a glimpse of that plan even as God prepared me to acknowledge my call.

So, what happens to our dreams? Too often life happens. We get so busy with the day-to-day grind we forget the dreams. Sometimes routine has us bogged down, and we have no time to remember. Reconnecting is an act of remembrance, a kind of anamnesis, a spiritual practice that involves actively remembering God's saving grace given to us through Jesus Christ.

In Luke 22:19, we see the institution of an anamnesis when Jesus established the Lord's Supper. The Scripture reads: "Then he took a loaf of bread, and when he had given thanks, he broke it and gave it to them, saying, 'This is my body, which is given for you. Do this in remembrance of me.'" Anamnesis through Communion is the practice of remembering the work of Jesus Christ in our salvation. It is a personal experience when we are encouraged to recall that Christ died for us so we might be saved. Through anamnesis, we reconnect with our experience of salvation through partaking of the bread and cup; in that act of remembrance we relive the experience as though it were the present time. Of particular importance in this reconnection is that we practice it mindfully.

Part of being mindful in our reconnecting is resisting the urge to condemn ourselves for losing touch with our dreams. As in the process of review, there is no condemnation in reconnecting. It is a reality of life: we lose touch with our dreams at times. We forget our assignment and lose our way for a while. However, this is why reconnection is so important. We need to make the time and space to go back and relive our experiences of call.

How did you feel when God called you? How did you feel when you were called to your first church? How did you feel when you got the job? Were you excited? Were you scared? What were your hopes and dreams for the role? What was it God told you to do? Whom did you involve as you developed your plans and strategies? How did you engage others?

Posing these questions is like turning over soil that has crusted over. We break up the fallow ground to aerate the soil and make what was hard arable. During aeration, we generate excitement: we recall our assignment, our plans, our dreams. We have the opportunity to use those dreams to inspire us anew. They can help us to reorient ourselves so we can set our sights on more hopeful possibilities.

Scriptural Grounding for Reconnecting

In reconnecting with the experience of being in relationship with God, we recognize the need to get back to God's plan for our lives. Consider the words of the psalmist, which The Message renders in this way:

> When I took a long, careful look at your ways, I got my feet back on the trail you blazed. I was up at once, didn't drag my feet, was quick to follow your orders. The wicked hemmed me in—there was no way out—but not for a minute did I forget your plan for me. I get up in the middle of the night to thank you; your decisions are so right, so true—I can't wait till morning! (Psalm 119:59-62)

The psalmist reflects on the plan God has for his life and realizes this divine plan is like a map to guide his actions. In fact, in the realization, the psalmist is anxious to get back on track. God's decisions for the psalmist are so right and true, he simply must stay on the path.

There is also a sense of energy and urgency associated with the passage. The psalmist is excited about getting back on the path God has for him. In the reconnecting, the psalmist recognizes he has strayed from the path and must return.

We see this same urgent need to return to the right path in the parable of the prodigal son, as recorded in Luke 15:11-32. We remember the story of a man with two sons, the younger of which demanded his portion of his father's wealth. Going off to a distant country, the younger son quickly spent all of his money, and landing on hard times, he was assigned to the fields to slop hogs. He was so hungry he would have eaten the corn cobs thrown out to the pigs, but no one gave him anything.

The son had strayed from the path and forgotten himself in his effort to go his own way. This happens to us sometimes. We get caught up in the day-to-day. We want to strike out on our own and create our own path. We become detached from our source and strength because we are busy doing the work. We fixate on the details rather than look up for inspiration.

In the case of the prodigal son, the Bible says he came to himself and remembered—reconnected to—who he was. He was his father's son. Even his father's hired hands had plenty of food to eat. All he needed to do was return to the path and plan his father had for him and he would be all right. The same is true for us. When we reconnect with God's call and plan for us, we regain our footing.

But reconnecting is more than regaining our footing. To reconnect is to rekindle. Second Timothy 1:6 says to us, "Rekindle the gift of God that is within you through the laying on of hands." In our call, God has equipped us and made alive in us what we need to accomplish our tasks. Reconnecting helps us by stirring us up so we can reach back into the recesses of our minds, remember the plans and dreams, and rekindle the excitement anew.

And again, in reconnecting, there is no need for condemnation and fear. As the writer of 2 Timothy 1:7 says, "God did not give us a spirit of cowardice, but rather a spirit of power and of love and of self-discipline." With this power, love, and soundness of mind, we can boldly reconnect to and reclaim what may have been lost, gaining strength from our reclamation.

What happens when we reconnect to those dreams? In 1 Kings 3, Solomon encountered God through a dream. In the dream, God instructed Solomon to ask for what he wanted as he took his place as Israel's king. Because Solomon asked for wisdom rather than long life, wealth, or the life of his enemies, God gave him not only great wisdom, but also riches and honor—things that he did not request. When Solomon woke from his dream, he was astounded. He knew it was a dream, but he felt an overwhelming sense of joy and gratitude. Solomon experienced a rush of emotions that affirmed the Spirit of God had filled him and prepared him for the office to which he was called.

Certainly, Solomon had not lost touch with the dream because it had just occurred. Yet, in waking he had an experience of reconnecting—remembering what he had dreamed and what God had told him. As he allowed himself to remember, Solomon was excited and grateful. The Message captures his sense of awe and gratitude wonderfully in 1 Kings 3:15. It reads: "Solomon woke up—what a dream!" What a dream, indeed. Reconnecting to the dream not only affirmed his ministry, but it also prepared him to go after it.

Reconnecting also helps us to recognize when we have completed what God has called us to do. In 2 Timothy 4:6-7, the writer is looking back over his life, recognizing it is at its end. He says, "As for me, I am already being poured out as a libation, and the time of my departure has come. I have fought the good fight, I have finished the race, I have kept the faith." This reflection has an element of reconnection. The writer recognized his current status and imminent death. By the same token, however, he acknowledged he had completed his assignment. He did what God called him to do and in his realization he was at peace. He knew God's reward for him was a crown of righteousness. Not just for him, but for every one who had similarly persevered. By reconnecting we can remember our callings and recognize our release from the assignment when the work is done.

What Pastoral Leaders Say about Reconnecting

Reconnecting has done several things for the leaders with whom I spoke. Many described a sense of reconnecting to their youth. One leader put it this way:

> The biggest feeling for me is getting reconnected to life and a certain part of my life that I associate with being youthful, more free and creative. So when I'm walking with music—music that I really like—it is . . . you feel a little bit more alive. And you feel like

> a part of you that maybe you lost because you're so busy working for so many years . . . the hope, that kind of the enthusiasm for living that you had, or you remember having as a younger person, you feel like you're tapping into it.

This leader remembered younger days when he felt free to dream, free to engage in youthful exuberance, and more creative as a result of that capacity to dream. Reconnecting was the opportunity to latch on to his younger self and dream.

We can all remember the uninhibited feeling of youth when our dreams had no limits, when we believed we had the ability to single-handedly change the world, and the indomitable spirit that rose up within us as a result of those dreams. We start our careers with that kind of fearless excitement and exuberance, before we heard "No" countless times.

We had such enthusiasm before we heard our share of "Oh, we don't do it that way here," or "We tried that once and it didn't work." Reconnecting allows us to strip away the layers of "No" and "It can't be done." It allows us to remember a time when our mantra was "Yes, we can."

That was the sense expressed by this leader, and the spark in his eyes demonstrated he could absolutely reconnect to those memories. It was immediately reminiscent of Psalm 37:25. I imagine David as an elder statesman, wizened by age, but not dimmed in faith. I see his eyes sparkle as he asserts, "I have been young, and now am old, yet I have not seen the righteous forsaken or their children begging bread." David expressed the excitement from reconnecting and his excitement is infectious because it engenders hope and optimism.

As I listened to this pastoral leader share, I wondered whether reconnecting resulted in part from lament. Specifically, I wondered if reconnecting to past dreams gave rise to misgivings about having allowed time to slip by and potential opportunities to pass. When I asked the question, this leader immediately refuted such an idea.

Although he acknowledged dreams had become a casualty as a result of marriage, having children, and career pursuits, he also recognized reconnecting enabled him to rekindle those dreams. For him, this was a source of great excitement and joy because he felt emboldened to dream again; to dust off those hopes and reorient himself to achieve his dreams. Of that process of reconnecting and rekindling he said, "It's almost like I'm saying 'Hey, maybe it's time to figure out how to get reengaged in that.'" Reconnecting resulted in a renewed excitement and it did not matter how old the dreams were or how long they had lain dormant.

As a result of rekindling, other leaders expressed the ability to connect with self. One leader said, "It's connecting to your own spirit . . . [and] connecting to the forces of the universe." It was as though the reconnecting resulted in a stripping away so the true self reemerges. Reconnecting allowed this leader to become reacquainted with who she was and the hopes that accompanied that true self. Yet, her reconnecting was not a selfish endeavor. Rather, through reconnecting, this leader saw herself in context with her place in the universe. Not only was this a spiritual phenomenon, but it was also incredibly meaningful and moving.

Another ministerial leader expressed a similar sentiment as he thought about reconnecting. Remembering the sovereignty and greatness of God, he referenced Psalm 90:4 which says, "For a thousand years in your sight are like yesterday when it is past, or like a watch in the night." For him the psalm was a reminder that we are just specks in comparison to God. We come, we go, and our lives are very short, but God is eternal. For this leader, reconnecting filled him with awe for a great and powerful God who exists from everlasting to everlasting, yet is still mindful of us. Reconnecting allows us to remember this as well.

Reconnecting, then, allows us as leaders to rekindle past dreams to become reacquainted with our more hopeful selves, while seeing ourselves in relationship with an awesome God. For me, this realization brings to mind Ephesians 3:20, "Now to him who by the power at work within us is able to accomplish abundantly far more than all we can ask or imagine. . . ." In remembering our dreams, we realize our dreams do not have to be limited because God is able to do so much more in us than we can even begin to request. That realization is absolutely critical.

As one leader noted, "How can I tell these people? How can I help them to understand unless they really believe that our God is a healing God who can transform, will transform, and pleasures in transforming?" For this leader, reconnecting allowed her to remember the miraculous healing power of God in her life. Then she was able, in turn, to exhort and call forth a greater faith in the people with whom she ministered. By reconnecting, not only had she been reenergized, but she energized others by increasing their faith.

Hebrews 11:1 exhorts, "Now faith is the assurance of things hoped for, the conviction of things not seen." Thus, as this leader discovered, those we serve become participants in their own healing by faith, a faith increased when we as their leaders reconnect to our experiences with a loving God.

Why Do We Need to Reconnect?

We need to reconnect because we too often forget. We forget the specifics of God's call on our lives. We think we remember, but sometimes we remember only the aspects of what we want to do or what we believe needs to be done. By reconnecting we reacquaint ourselves with God's call and plan so we know what we must do and when we are done.

We need to reconnect because we forget the hopeful dreams we had in years past. I remember a pastor once asked my son what he wanted to be when he grew up. My son immediately responded that he would be the first pastor-astronaut to deliver his sermons from space. Who knows if that dream will ever come to fruition, but how remarkably ambitious is it? I hope my son never loses sight of such boldness, even though I know life and reality have a way of blunting the edges of our sharpened ideals. What great and wonderful dream did you once have? Perhaps you need to reconnect to reclaim it.

Finally, we need to reconnect to reenergize. The mundane aspects of ministry sometimes make us feel more like flightless turkeys than soaring eagles. Reconnecting helps us lift our sights to see beyond the day-to-day. When our sights are elevated, we find our energy elevated as well. New possibilities have a way of increasing our perspective. As we gain perspective, we release creative energy. What seemed impossible becomes a possibility, and we cannot help but become excited as a result.

That is the heart of the hope inspired by Ephesians 3:20. God is able to do so much more than we can possibly dream based on the power that works within us. Therefore, by reconnecting we stir up the dreams and increase our perspective. Reconnecting has the effect of increasing God's power in our lives because God is able to do even more than raise our perspective. Reconnecting is an exercise of faith, and like any other type of exercise, reconnecting produces an increase in that which it exercises—our faith.

What Can You Do to Reconnect?

As a consultant working with clients engaged in software application development projects, I led initial sessions that focused on helping our clients establish their mission and vision. Establishing a mission and vision requires an abstracted view—a detachment from negative impulses that serve to thwart dreaming. To free minds, I encouraged clients to imagine floating on the clouds. I encouraged them to visualize being high in the air, dreaming comfortably as the cottony softness of the fluffy cloud enveloped them. Effectively, the freeing imagery of clouds became like a guided meditation that made dreaming possible.

Reconnecting is like participating in a guided meditation: see yourself on a fluffy cloud. Can you visualize yourself floating away and dreaming without limits or restraints? In experiencing such freedom, where do your dreams take you? How do such dreams make you feel? What thoughts, emotions, and plans are renewed in you as you dream freely?

To reconnect is to remember your hopeful self, who had great plans and dreams. This is the chance to be once more an emboldened being who faithfully and fearlessly reaches out to seize opportunities to bring those dreams to fruition. That is the invitation to reconnect. Thus, the question becomes, what can you do to reconnect?

Engaging in a guided meditation is one way. As I write, I am looking at my lounge chair and prayer shawl. I cannot help but think of the days when I curl up in that chair, wrap my shawl around my shoulders, close my eyes, and let my mind wander until I rise like fluffy clouds overhead. From the comfort of that chair, I guide my thoughts in a meditative prayer, and I remember God's call on my life. As I think back on those times, remembering all of the particulars about my call, I am inspired and excited. I can rest in those thoughts with a blessed assurance that God's hand is upon me.

Another way to reconnect is through walking. Something about movement is reminiscent of reconnection. Imagine as you walk that you are stepping into God's plan for your life. With each step, see yourself moving toward the goals and strategies that need to be developed and implemented in order for that divine plan to come to fruition. Are you trudging up an incline? Think of the strength God has given you to persevere. Is the path you're walking paved or uneven, gravel or riddled with roots and rocks? How does the path itself and the care needed to navigate it seem analogous to your life's journey? Consider how God has smoothed rough places or removed obstacles along life's path. In reconnecting through such movement, we can experience a sense of spiritual progress as we move physically.

Perhaps you reconnect to yourself and God through nature. Many leaders described walking in the woods, sitting near the water, or riding a bike through tree-canopied streets. There is something about creation that helps us reconnect to God even as we reconnect to ourselves. It can be an awe-inspiring experience, evoking a sense of knowing that through God all things are possible.

Do whatever it is that helps you to reconnect. Regardless of your method, reconnect with hope and wonder, as one who rekindles a possible dream and not with lament or condemnation as one who has lost the chance. By the grace of God, we have new mercies every day. Therefore, we have new chances to reconnect to our dreams, God's call, and the ministry God has for our lives. We simply need to reconnect to reclaim what God has for us.

So What?

Remember how I described walking through the darkened halls of the church where I accepted the call to serve, and how I heard the voice of the Lord say, "Reclaim my church"? It has been in reconnecting with that memory myself that I better understood what God intended for me to do. I was like the pastor who believed her call was to turn the church around. When I came to the congregation, there were no activities through which the church ministered to the neighboring community. On Sunday, we held worship services. On Tuesday, the church doors were open for church meetings, and on Thursday for choir rehearsals. Otherwise, the church building sat closed and locked to the community.

We did rent space in the building, but fearing the loss of rental income, we attempted to make the available space generic so as not to offend the renter. It was wholly possible to walk in the church facility, but never see the name of the church or information about its ministries prominently displayed anywhere.

Through reconnecting I began to recognize what God intended for us to offer. The Lord wanted us to minister more as the body of Jesus Christ, where neighborhood residents and businesses would perceive our church as a community hub. To that end, we began opening our doors for more community activities. I wanted to see our church bustling seven days a week to such an extent that people would drive by and say, "What's going on at the Baptist church?"

More than that, we became intentional about displaying church information—our purpose, mission, times of worship, informational brochures, and business cards—so there was no mistaking who we were and the purpose of our ministry. We hosted teen rock bands and New Year's Eve celebrations. We hosted classes in Zumba and ballroom dancing. And we made sure that, as community groups came to the church, they did more than simply rent space in a generic facility. Those groups came to know we were a house of faith, and we became community partners once more.

As I reconnected with my past, I remembered God's call to me and was able to follow God's plan faithfully. What was remarkable was how God placed the opportunities right in front of us. People came to us wanting to connect. We did not have to market ourselves in any particular way or be forceful in our outreach efforts. We simply leveraged the opportunities God gave us to serve, and those opportunities became obvious when we took the moment to see what God was doing in our midst.

Abram heard God say, "Go to a land I will show you." Similarly, God showed my congregation a way of being in community that would allow us to reconnect and make a bigger impact than we could with our doors closed and locked to the public. Reconnecting is an invitation. It is the opportunity to remember once again God's call and go forward in that call, expecting that God will make firm our steps as we go.

Reconnecting is remembering God has a plan for us and realizing that plan is exceedingly and abundantly greater than all we can ask or imagine. We only need to go get it. Reconnecting is being reenergized and renewed by dreams still in our grasp.

As we reconnect, we become excited and empowered. We become emboldened and courageous. As we reconnect, we are free to dream again of the possibilities and bolstered with the thought: "Hey, maybe it is time to figure out how to reengage with that."

Questions to Consider

1. What do you remember about your call to ministry? How was God present in your call? Take time now to reconnect with the heart of what God called you to do.
2. In response to your call, what plans and dreams did you develop? Write them down as you remember.
3. Review the list of dreams and plans you once held. As you read through these plans, what speaks to you now? Which item is particularly moving or draws your focus and energy? Why?
4. As you reconnect to God's call on your life, do you discern there is still work to be done, or do you realize you have finished your assignment?
5. What Scriptures speak to you regarding reconnection? How might you engage those Scriptures now in your journey?

·8·

reflect

Yet they did not obey or incline their ear, but, in the stubbornness of their evil will, they walked in their own counsels, and looked backward rather than forward. (Jeremiah 7:24)

WHAT DOES IT mean to reflect? Researchers Chris Argyris and Donald Schön, from Harvard University and Massachusetts Institute of Technology (MIT) respectively, submitted that "all human beings . . . need to become competent in taking action and simultaneously reflecting on this action to learn from it."[1] They contend this ability to move forward while looking back to assess past actions is the basis of the practice of reflecting. If they are correct, then the Scripture from the prophet Jeremiah represents the antithesis of reflection!

God speaks through Jeremiah to launch a divine complaint against Israel. Rather than reflecting upon the faithfulness of God and remembering that faithfulness to propel for forward action, the people of Israel operated out of their volition and will. God heard the cries of the Israelites and faithfully freed them from the hands of the Egyptians. Then, God promised that if Israel was obedient and remained faithful, God would in turn be faithful to them.

118 spiritual practices for effective leadership

Israel was called to consider God's acts in their lives through reflection and remembering. The Lord expected the people to observe and discern the difference between positive outcomes that resulted from obedience and negative outcomes that resulted from disobedience. Through this ability to discern, Israel would have been equipped to live as a faithful people. They would have been better able to do those things that were pleasing to God.

However, the people of Israel did not heed the prophet's urging. Israel did not reflect on God's goodness or use reflective learning to direct the path of its people. Israel's history was strewn with willfully determined acts that were contrary to God's demand. They were intent on going their own way and determined to enact their own plan, including making sacrifices to the Babylonian goddess Ishtar, the "Queen of Heaven" (Jeremiah 7:18-24). The failure to look back and reflect on their disobedient actions, particularly in contrast with God's past faithfulness, resulted ultimately in divine judgment against the nation and its people.

To reflect is to learn from the past in order to redirect our efforts and move forward in more productive and positive ways in the future. It is a process of association whereby, through remembering, we call forth past experiences. Then, we combine that knowledge with an assessment of a current reality to chart a course in keeping with the synthesis of past experience and existing reality. Ideally, this process helps us learn and move forward in life-giving and faithful ways.

For example, have you ever cautioned a child, or perhaps been cautioned as a child, "The stove is hot! Don't touch or you'll get burned"? Often children do not heed such warning. Some are curious; some are obstinate; some do not understand the instruction or the consequences. These children invariably touch the stove, only to experience an injury in the process. In most cases, it only takes one touch to cement the lesson. If the situation repeats itself, the same child, having been warned again that the stovetop is hot, will reflect on the previous experience of being burned and will not touch the stove again.

This kind of learning, based on experience, is time and again gained as children grow and mature. Human beings have the capacity to remember a past experience, combine that knowledge with a current reality, and use that past experience to ensure a more positive encounter in the present. Regrettably, as leaders, we don't always pause to reflect on the increasingly complex experiences to identify past cause-and-effect relationships in order to improve present circumstances. If we will take time to engage the process of reflection, we will gain competence as past learning drives faithful action.

The Need for Reflection

Let's pause now to reflect on this evolving 7 Rs process. Review reminds us to look at our current work and consider it in the scope of our present activities. Reconnecting reminds us to look at the call on our lives and identify once more the tasks God has given us to do. Now the work is to bring the focus of our review and reconnection efforts together in a way that empowers us to move faithfully into the future. This is what we do when we reflect. As people of faith, the process of remembering God's faithfulness in the past emboldens us for greater trust and movement toward the future.

I think about my call from corporate leadership to pastoral ministry. It was a frightening transition. For one, a corporate executive makes significantly more money than most pastors. I remember sitting in a church administration course during my Master of Divinity studies. The professor, who was also a pastor, spoke of the small salary afforded for pastoral ministry. My first thought was, "I'll never be a pastor." How could someone possibly pay bills or meet obligations on such a small salary?

I also harbored fears about pastoral ministry itself. I knew how to be a technologist, but what did I know about being a pastor? Was I really prepared for ministry? When I was called to serve a church while still in seminary, I was close to panic. How would I possibly manage all of the things I did not yet know how to do?

Truly I needed to engage in reflection to embolden my steps. I needed to remember God had been with me when I graduated from college and moved 1,000 miles from home to begin a career as a software engineer. I had to remember God had blessed and kept me through the lean years of establishing myself professionally and personally in that new environment. I had to remember God had been a constant presence and help through all situations.

Having those experiences as touchstones in my life, I was able to look at my current situation in a new light. Certainly, I was concerned about finances and my level of preparation. However, if God had been with me through secular endeavors, why did I fear God would not be with me when I was answering this new call God had placed on my life? And so, I was emboldened to go forward in faith. I was emboldened with the belief that I would be fine. More than that, I came to believe I had the ability to thrive.

This is my testimony. My finances were secure; I never missed a bill payment. There was money enough to tithe faithfully and meet my obligations. Moreover, being in seminary when I assumed my pastorate was an unexpected blessing. Whenever I had a question in ministry, my mentors and professors were on hand to help me. God graciously gave me what I needed to respond with preparedness to my calling. I reflected on past experiences and felt strengthened through the reflection, which emboldened my trust of God. The result? I was no longer afraid going forward.

Of course, there is more to this process of reflection. It is a generative cycle. In reflection, we remember past examples of God's faithfulness in our lives, which can motivate our present actions. In turn, such faithful action today becomes part of a faithful past that strengthens us anew for future action. We do not traverse a circle of reflection only once. As the lyrics of the hymn "Great Is Thy Faithfulness" convey, we have strength for today and bright hope for tomorrow. Reflection creates an upward spiral of remembrance and forward movement.

So, for my experience of reflection, I remember what God has done for me. I remember the grace shown to me as I moved through my transition. I remember God's provisions, through finances and the wise counsel that aided and guided me. Such remembrance reinforces my trust in God. As such, I can draw upon that remembrance to propel and prepare me for future challenges.

So now, when I face a transition, I recognize I am in a different place spiritually, physically, mentally, and emotionally, which means the parameters of the current transition are not the same as transitions of the past. And yet, I can draw upon lessons learned and strength gained in the past. I do not have to experience the same scenario to be emboldened for new challenges. I can remember how God was with me in the past and how God brought me through the uncertain times.

Therefore, when I face times of diminishing or scarce resources, even if those times are new and unfamiliar, I remember how God was my provider in the past. When I need counsel, even if the counsel is for a new challenge, I remember God has always provided teachers as my situations required. And through reflection, my intentional remembrance enables me to face future challenges.

That is what reflection should stir in each of us. When Moses asked God in Exodus 3 about God's name and what to say to the Children of Israel, God said, "Tell them I AM has sent me to you." Reflection reminds us God's word to us is as true as God's word was to Moses. God is the "I Am" who provides what we need, when we need it, according to God's perfect will. We do well to remember what God has done for us and to reflect on those memories as milestones to guide us faithfully forward. The lessons we learn from reflection help us to increase our faith and realize greater trust in God through our Lord and Savior, Jesus Christ.

What Is Reflection?

Reflection combines ideas from the researchers Argyris and Schön with our experiences as people of faith. Argyris and Schön encourage competence in the ability to take action and simultaneously reflect on it in order to learn from it. Scripture encourages us to remember the faithfulness of God and use that recollection to encourage faithful action for the future. Bringing these ideas together, spiritual reflection requires us to consider a current situation while simultaneously remembering God's faithful actions in the past, so that we might be strengthened in our remembrance. Then we may be able to act in faithful, courageous, and forward-moving ways in keeping with God's goodness and grace in our lives.

Specifically, reflection calls us first to consider our present context and situation, which we mindfully remembered during review. Recall that in review we became aware of the disparate parts and pieces of our leadership context. We remembered what is happening in our ministry, including the goals and objectives we may have set for ourselves and our congregations. In review, we acknowledged multiple and often conflicting demands, asking God to help us be discerning about the priorities of those demands, without anxiety or self-condemnation for whatever we may identify as neglected or forgotten. In reflecting now on all those concerns, we must endeavor to remain meditative, nonjudgmental, and focused—open to what God may seek to teach us through consideration of the present.

Second, reflection calls us to look backward to examine the original goals and ideals that came to mind during the process of reconnection. In reconnecting we intentionally remembered the call God placed on our lives. We needed to engage in that time of reconnecting, lest we become consumed by the routine and lose touch with those initial dreams and forget a sense of our calling. As we reconnected, we gave ourselves permission to dream and remember anew the experience of God calling our name. In this process also, we resisted the temptation to condemn ourselves for what may seem like a loss of focus or an unhelpful detour in our pursuit of the call. The greater travesty would be not revisiting those hopes and dreams at all. Therefore, we intentionally reconnected to reacquaint ourselves with our dreams and to determine whether those dreams still hold promise for us. Part of reflection is to look back on that initial call and what we discovered about our former dreams.

However, the process of reflection requires an additional step. Reflection requires weaving and integration. It is as if we hold the tasks acknowledged in review in one hand while grasping the ideas remembered in reconnecting in the other. Our job in reflection is to weigh the present and past, comparing and contrasting to identify any gaps and disconnects between our current work and our original calling.

Does your current work relate to your calling? Are you living out your dreams and the desires of your heart in what you do? Based on your original call, have you finished your assignment? What more may you be called to do? These are the types of questions asked in reflection, for it is necessary to accomplish the integrating and weaving work of this R. Reflection is, in fact, a lot like braiding.

My son has been growing out his hair for the last several years. That presents me with a challenge as his mother. You see, my family always joked that I should have a son because I never had the knack for combing and styling long hair, not even in my childhood years of playing dolls. Now that my son has achieved a fairly significant length in his own hair, each month I take him to a professional stylist to have his hair braided in cornrows.

For the uninitiated, a cornrow is a braiding process in which three sections of hair are woven together, while progressively integrating additional sections of hair into the woven braid. The result is a braid that remains closely attached the scalp. I can *describe* the process, but I am completely unable to do it. As I watched my son's stylist work, however, I could not help but recognize the parallels of reflection.

Reviewing and reconnecting are the first two sections of hair, but without reflection as the third section, the braid will not hold together. We remember the current context in the process of review. We remember our call, hopes, and dreams in the process of reconnecting. But then we weave those remembrances together with reflection.

I envision taking one section in my fingers as I think about the present goals and objectives I have set. I cross it with another section as I recall what God first called me to do. When I weave in the third section, I am compelled to look closely at my current context and my past call to see if the first two are aligned or if I have gotten off course.

That initial crossing over of three sections produces a simple braid, which is fine, but that is not how one achieves a cornrow. To cornrow, I must integrate additional strands of hair, picking up each new section and weaving it together with the preceding to create the tightly woven row of this long-lasting braid.

Reflection allows us to create a similarly complex and tightly woven integration of present and past to consider the interwoven nature of our experiences of God. We remember how God provided for us in the midst of a challenging situation, and we integrate the reflection into the braid. We remember how God gave us the counsel to offer when we spoke to someone in the midst of a crisis, and then we weave that into the braid as well. With each remembrance, we incorporate those experiences of God into the braid as we reflect. By doing so, we remain close to the source, who is God, just as the experienced stylist remains close to the scalp with a cornrow.

This analogy offers additional points of comparison with the practice of reflection. Integrating sections of hair into the braid is just one part of creating a cornrow. The stylist's hands must move with skill and dexterity while braiding in order to make forward progression and to complete each row. What's more, it takes more than a single row to encompass a full head of hair. Depending on the thickness of the sections selected, a person's head may have dozens of rows of finely braided hair before the stylist is done.

Similarly, reflection requires movement as we go through the process. Having crossed over the first three sections, we are equipped to move along the row of the braid, propelled by increasing urgency and inspiration as we recognize where we are on track or where we may have deviated from the path. Both of these assessments can be energizing.

When we realize our current goals are in keeping with our call, then we are encouraged to keep doing what we are doing. When we realize we are not where we expected to be, then we have the opportunity to determine whether a new approach or tactic is required. To keep with the analogy of the braid, do we need to straighten the row or allow the unexpected curve to continue following the natural contours of the head? Engaging in this kind of reflective reassessment helps us to make forward, faithful progress.

Each cycle of reflection is like a completed cornrow on my son's head. Having reached the end of the row, the stylist has the opportunity to flex his or her fingers and assess the progress thus far. The process is far from complete, but each time we pause to weave together our review and reconnection in the practice of reflection, we create a new source of testimony to God's presence has been with us.

With each braided row of reflection, we also recognize the reality of change and movement in life—and the need for such movement. We do not stand still in our lives. We may encounter similar situations, but the specific circumstances are different. In each movement of life, we face new circumstances and new challenges, despite the occasional sense of experiencing déjà vu.

Pastoral ministry has this kind of dynamic annually. We look at the church year and recognize it is cyclical as we go through the seasons of the year. Yet, each year brings different challenges.

✦   It is Christmas and the church has always hosted a breakfast with Santa, but with the church in decline, fewer people are available to help and all the children in the congregation have grown up.

+ The church is increasing in membership, and you want to bring some new members to the table for Lenten planning. How do you do this without alienating long-term members?

+ The church has always been a haven for new immigrant groups in the community, but now recognizes it cannot serve the newest group of immigrants without partnering with another church.

Each scenario has familiar aspects, but current realities infuse new challenges. That is the reality of pastoral ministry. Yet, the psalmist declared in Psalm 34:19, "Many are the afflictions of the righteous, but the LORD rescues them from them all." God provided resources in the past to do the work to which we were called; the same God will provide the means today. Circumstances change and our ministry methods may need to change in response, but God remains unchanging and faithful.

It is this realization and remembrance that emboldens us to act courageously in a faithful and forward way. It is the way of reflection: we take an action and simultaneously reflect on it, remembering the move of God in our lives. In this way, we not only learn from our past and present, but we also determine how to move forward.

Scriptural Grounding for Reflection

The Bible provides a number of references that speak of reflection. Throughout the Scriptures, we are called to remember God's acts of faithfulness toward humanity. Scripture also calls us to remember God's commandments. By remembering God's grace and precepts, we, in turn, are empowered to act and move according to that remembrance.

As this chapter suggested at the start, reflection requires the ability to recognize God's hand in our lives and experiences. By recognizing the move of God, we are motivated to act in a way that demonstrates our faith in God.

This was not the case depicted in Jeremiah 7:24. The people of Israel failed to recognize they would incur the wrath of God for failing to obey faithfully in response to God's grace and favor. The prophet Daniel offered this same warning in his time when he said, "Just as it is written in the law of Moses, all this calamity has come upon us. We did not entreat the favor of the LORD our God, turning from our iniquities and reflecting on his fidelity" (Daniel 9:13). The people did not engage in reflection, using remembrance of God's goodness to guide faithful, future actions. Instead, they went their own way and experienced what Daniel called calamity.

Psalm 77 illustrates both aspects of reflection: taking action while looking back. Moreover, the psalmist remembers God's faithfulness to inspire forward progress. The psalm begins in grief and sorrow, with the psalmist asking if he will ever see God's faithful acts again in his life. His current situation is calamity; he is disheartened. It is the act of reflection that serves to change his perspective. Verse 11 declares remembrance of the deeds of the Lord and the miracles of long ago. In remembering, he reflects on all God has done, meditating on God's actions. That sequence of events—remembering and reflecting—enables the psalmist to declare with certainty that God's ways are holy. As he remembers the works of God, his lament gives way to praise. The practice of reflection bolsters his faith and confidence, enabling him to weather a difficult storm.

In Psalm 119, the idea of reflecting on God's law and ways is prominent. For example, in verse 15 the psalmist says reflecting on God's law makes him happy. In verse 23 he acknowledges that, even though influential people plot against him, reflecting on God's law is a delight. By understanding God's commands, he is better able to reflect on God's miracles and thereby be sustained even in the midst of grief. As he reflects on God's word, he is comforted. Even though people mock him, reflecting on God's word has been his source of hope (v. 50). Whether he is dealing with arrogant people who tell lies about him or pining away the hours through a sleepless night, the psalmist engages in reflection in God's law. To him, it is a source of strength.

So, according to the psalmist, the history of God's people as recorded in Scripture may be part of the past on which we reflect. Our faith is not rooted solely in our personal experiences, of course, but also in the community of faith through the generations. God's word becomes sustenance during times of trouble, helping us remember that we have not been the first to endure ridicule or suffering or temptation. The history of our families, of our congregation, of our denomination may also provide encouragement as we remember how God has moved in that shared past to provide for God's people. This is the power of reflection's dual backward and forward focus.

There is yet another component in the practice of reflection, one that suggests a perfecting aspect in the process. In chapter 3 of this volume, I introduced spirituality as a process whereby an individual corrects his or her life, patterning self against an ideal. For pastoral leaders, the Scriptures point to Jesus Christ as our ideal.

Consider 2 Corinthians 3:18, which says, "And all of us, with unveiled faces, seeing the glory of the Lord as though reflected in a mirror, are being transformed into the same image from one degree of glory to another; for this comes from the Lord, the Spirit." Not only are we freed by the Spirit to view the glory of God unveiled, as revealed in Jesus, but we ourselves reflect that glory as we are transformed into a reflection of Jesus, our ideal.

This text is taken from a larger passage that describes Moses, who was compelled to cover his face after an encounter with God on the mountaintop, so blinding was even the reflected glory of that experience. However, over time the glory began to fade. In contrast, Paul notes that through Jesus Christ the reflected glory of God does not dim. Rather, the trajectory of our patterned actions moves us from glory to glory.

This is a stunning metaphor for the spiritual practice of reflection. Through patterning of our lives after Jesus, we are corrected and perfected in pursuit of our ideal. We know we will not achieve perfection until we are glorified; yet, we achieve greater degrees of glory as we press toward the mark which is the high calling of Jesus Christ. In the gradual process through which we reflect on the example of Jesus, we rely on the guidance of the Holy Spirit to move us closer to our ideal—in effect, to become a reflection (the mirror image) of the One on whom we reflect.

This mirror-image understanding of reflection is echoed in Philippians 1:27 where Paul exhorted the believers, "Live as citizens who reflect the Good News about Christ. Then, whether I come to see you or whether I stay away, I'll hear all about you. I'll hear that you are firmly united in spirit, united in fighting for the faith that the Good News brings."[2] In this verse Christians are encouraged to live as people who reflect the gospel of Jesus Christ, seeking to live as he lived.

If others are able to see Christ in us, doesn't it seem reasonable to believe we have engaged in the process of reflection? Specifically, we have taken action, remembering the person and example of Jesus so that, through the Holy Spirit, we are able to align with Christ as our ideal and reflect his image.

Paul fully expected that as the early Christians lived a life of Christ, people would talk about the love and unity among believers and he would hear about their example because it was so counter-cultural! In a time of social division and strife, the example of a community united in love and common concern would be striking. And this is exactly what we are called to do as followers of Jesus Christ today. In a time when societal trends tempt us to choose sides and do whatever is most expeditious, reflection becomes the means by which we stay on course. We take action in the current context and reflect not only on our personal experiences with God, but also on God's faithful move throughout scriptural history. Then, to truly move forward in the way God would have us go, we must pattern our action after our ideal, who is Jesus Christ, relying on the Holy Spirit's leading and guidance to attain that ideal.

Taken together, the Old and New Testaments point us to reflection. The Old Testament helps us look back at both God's faithfulness and humanity's persistence in seeking its own way. Through reflection, we remember and learn something about God and about ourselves. In the New Testament, God gives us the Son as the ideal after which we can pattern our lives. Through reflection, we remember Jesus' life among us and anticipate his return, and we take action to model our lives after his. This is the backward and forward engagement that reflection encourages.

What Pastoral Leaders Say about Reflection

One leader shared with me about how she regularly and intentionally seeks time apart for reflection and renewal. She added that taking time to think through, pray about, and ponder especially difficult issues is very helpful for her. This leader, an executive of a faith-based organization, described the challenges she faced as she tried to bring renewal to an organization in need of change.

She was new in her job but well-qualified for the reorganizational task she was called to perform. She found the organization had drifted from its mission and needed to shed real estate, people, and practices not core to the organization's charter. Yet having to shed resources, including people, is incredibly difficult.

As many faith-based, nonprofit organizations can attest, the organizational culture had become a family. Even when it became obvious that practices had to change if the organization were to survive, people were reticent about making changes. This leader carried the weight and burden of helping the organization realize a sustainable future and struggled with the overwhelming demands of being the leader called to lead change.

To bolster her in these challenging times, this leader spent a good amount time in prayer and reflection on her role as a leader. She knew such time apart was critical for her leadership because the temptation was to move slowly or tinker around organizational edges, not pressing for the type of deep change she knew needed to occur. She needed courage to promote and push for such change. The practice of reflection equipped her with that courage. In reflection, she was able to review her current context and the challenges it presented while reviewing the call to lead the organization at a critical time. Reflection brought these remembrances into full view and consideration so she felt empowered to do what was necessary, regardless of the difficulty and unpopularity of her decisions.

Nevertheless, like many leaders, she admitted she did not engage in this practice of reflection frequently enough. She said, "I sometimes wish that I did this kind of practice more frequently than I do. I tend to engage in that kind of silent, quiet reflection only in times of crisis."

This is one of the challenges in reflection. Implied in the practice is taking time to engage. So often in leadership we are convinced that we need to be doing something, that our inactivity is not productive. But reflection is a thoughtful process that requires time apart to review, reconnect, and then reflect prior to action. In fact, we do ourselves a disservice as leaders when we only engage during times of crisis because we tend to become too self-reliant rather than relying on God's leading in our lives. We need to make space to engage in daily reflection. If we do this, we become better able to remain on the path representing God's plan and will for our lives.

Another leader spoke of reflection as a regular practice. He gets up each morning, has a cup of coffee, and reflects. He relishes his time in isolation where he can reflect before starting the day. This time of reflection makes a difference in his pastoral leadership, making it possible to get through holy days of the faith when the demands of the ministry are so great. Most pastoral leaders will agree when we consider the busyness of Advent and Christmas and of Lent and Easter. Ministry in those seasons is full and demanding, and time to reflect, even over a cup of coffee, can bring a welcomed break to an otherwise busy schedule.

Another leader shared how the daily practice of reflection helped him in his ministry and in his personal life. He takes time every morning and evening for a period of reflection and meditation. That reflection time informs his daily life. Given the busyness of his work, the practice of reflection makes it possible to manage the stresses of a demanding schedule, but beyond that, he said reflection helps him maintain humility. So often in leadership, particularly when things are going well, we may believe we are the secret to our success. This leader used his reflection time to keep his ego in check and remember his reliance on God.

He also used reflection to ground him in his work. Reflection required him to ask, "Is the work I'm doing, is the work that I'm leading—is it an act of service?" For this leader, being called of God meant every activity needed to be an authentic representation of his faith life. During reflection he felt compelled to ask the question, "Who am I serving? Am I fooling myself to think somebody is being served?"

Such questions require a fair amount of reflection because the answers are not simple. Without time to reflect, leaders may be tempted to build up a fantasy world where we believe ourselves to be doing all the right things all in our own wisdom and strength. Through reflection it becomes possible to see the truth of our current situation and, in humility, to realign ourselves with God's call and purposes.

Why Do We Need to Reflect?

This book is about leadership effectiveness—how to be efficacious in leadership. This idea functions in two dimensions. Imagine a ball. The ball spins on its axis, which is the dimension of doing the right thing in leadership. That right thing is mobilizing a team to engage in the learning required to solve challenges that lack easy answers.

Effectiveness is a generative capacity, however. Thus, it is a ball that spins end over end, even as it rotates on its axis. In this dimension, effectiveness recognizes the work does not stop. Yesterday's challenges have been resolved and we address today's as well, but tomorrow brings us new challenges. Therefore, we cannot rest on our laurels as leaders. We must continue the effort to mobilize, encourage, and motivate our teams to achieve new heights. It is this combination of effectiveness in leadership that helps us to reach and exceed our goals.

Reflection helps leaders to achieve that multidimensional, generative capacity. It offers a process for taking action in concert with reflecting on that action, enabling us to learn even in the midst of our engagement. Again, we review our current context and the challenges confronting us, and we reconnect with God's call on our lives and the work we were given to do. Yet, reflection is not a one-for-one match as we bring forward the thoughts that arise when we review and reconnect.

For example I know God called me to serve as a pastor to pastors and to help ministerial leaders be more effective in the work God has called them to do. In my current role, I have an opportunity to live out my calling in many aspects of my work, some more obvious than others. In fact, I have a tendency to want to focus on the work that is clearly related to my call, such as when I am leading the retreat or conducting a workshop. However, the infrastructural and administrative tasks of my position make that other work possible. To ignore what often feel like less important activities would be harmful to the organization I serve and detrimental to me in living out my call.

Reflection has been the means by which I stay on track. By reviewing my current context, I see what lies ahead—and truth be told, the view can be overwhelming. The review helps me recognize what needs to occur and helps me remain grounded in the process. In reconnecting, I relive my call and remember what God has called me to do. Reconnection excites me anew. Then, reflection integrates past and present for the purpose of moving forward into the future. We need that spiritual practice to help us know how to proceed— and to inspire the courage we need to act.

Remember the leader who recognized her organization had drifted from its mission? She needed to make difficult and unpopular decisions for the organization's future and sustainability. Without reflection, she may have lost the nerve to do what she knew was necessary. Reflection did not make the job easier, but it did increase her resolve, which allowed her to recognize success by accomplishing the work to which God had called her.

What Can You Do to Reflect?

For me reflection is a visual process. I see the parts and pieces of my leadership context, having gone through review. I see them before me like petals of a flower laid out on display. Likewise, I relive the sights and sounds of my call. I see the people who were around me in the various stages of the emerging clarity of my call. And with those two sections of review and reconnection in hand, I imagine weaving and braiding the strands together so I can compare and contrast where I am now, what I am doing, and which activities relate to what God has called me to do.

Can you see yourself engaging in a similar practice? Sit and silently remember the process of review. What are the parts and pieces of your leadership? What do you find yourself doing on a daily, weekly, or monthly basis? What keeps you so busy and occupied? Breathe deeply in and out as you remember. This is not a time to feel overwhelmed by all you have to do; rather, it is the opportunity to put everything on the table to consider with God as your guide.

And then reconnect. Remember what you felt so passionately drawn to do. I remember years ago when I was wrestling with my call to ministry, and the theme song to the movie *Mahogany* played over the intercom system. I was walking through a store and heard the words. It was as though God was asking me whether I knew where I was going or what I was doing. As I listened to the song from the speakers, I remember looking up and saying, "All right God! I hear you!" What I took as God's not-so-subtle hint is a reminder forever etched in my brain. What reminds you of your call? Is it a memory, a song, an individual? Remember what God called you to and hold it before you.

In fact, see yourself holding the strands of memory together—the parts and pieces of your current context and your original call. See yourself interlacing those memories as if preparing to plait the strands of hair to form a braid. Cross one hand over the other, weaving them together and adding new strands and sections while you compare and contrast them together.

Are you living out your call? Are you honoring what is necessary? What changes need to be made that you have yet to implement? How might remembering God's past faithfulness in your life embolden you in your present and future work?

So What?

I heard a preacher suggest that if tomorrow were able to talk, it would remind us of God's promises. Inspired by Jeremiah's cry in the book of Lamentations, her sermon recounted how Jeremiah moaned his soul was without peace. His affliction was like wormwood and gall. Nevertheless, in the midst of his suffering, Jeremiah looked with hope for the future, recognizing that the God he served would honor God's promises.

Reflection is the opportunity to remember that the God we serve is faithful. God is a covenant keeper and we do not have to be afraid. We can look forward and know God will illumine our footsteps and make them firm.

No wonder, then, another leader noted reflection was as necessary as food for him. His daily opportunities for reflection, prayer, and meditation were as vital to his well-being as having regular meals. "And if you stop reflecting," he said, "it's like you stop feeding your soul." For him, not engaging in reflection was like spiritual starvation. He considered it a critical part of becoming a complete human being in this world.

These outcomes are in keeping with what leadership theorists espouse. The act of reflection makes it possible for leaders to regain a sense of purpose, determine what needs to be done, and return to the leadership context ready to reengage. The ability to reflect upon an action and learn from it helps us manage the dynamics of a changing environment. Reflection is the core capability for leadership efficacy because it helps us sharpen our impact as we attempt to mobilize and motivate others.

Questions to Consider

1. Leadership theorists Argyris and Schön maintain we must be competent in taking an action while simultaneously reflecting on that action to learn as we move forward. What

do you think of this assertion? What are examples in your life when you engaged in this kind of learning process?

2. When was the last time you sat to reflect on aspects of your leadership, ministry, or call? Is there a special place in which you engage in reflection? How might you make this practice a part of your daily habit?

3. Israel forgot God's faithfulness and failed to reflect on God's plan as they determined their future actions. We fall into the same neglect. Remember a time when God helped you through a challenging situation. How might that remembrance prepare you for a work you have to do?

4. What Scriptures help you to reflect? How do they support such reflection?

5. What ideas for review arose as you read this chapter?

NOTES

1. Chris Argyris and Donald A. Schön, *Theory in Practice: Increasing Professional Effectiveness* (San Francisco: Jossey-Bass, 1974), 4.

2. God's Word to the Nations Bible Society, Electronic Edition STEP Files. Copyright © 1998, Parsons Technology, Inc.

·9·

recalibrate

I know, O Lord, that the way of human beings is not in their control, that mortals as they walk cannot direct their steps. Correct me, O Lord, but in just measure; not in anger, or you will bring me to nothing. (Jeremiah 10:23-24)

DO YOU USE a global positioning system (GPS) for navigation purposes? Many of us do. Gone are the days when we keep badly folded maps in our glove compartment or use a travel service to provide precalculated routes. Gone are the days when we print out a simple piece of paper and try to negotiate turns while reading. Instead, we attach a pocket-sized device to a windshield or pull out our smartphones to enter the address of our destination and allow an automated voice to direct our every turn.

These GPS devices have made navigating unfamiliar places so much easier. However, the devices can also be incredibly annoying, particularly if you happen to miss a turn. As though silent alarm bells have been set off, the automated voice declares, "Recalculating, recalculating!" You cannot help but feel chastised as the system adjusts to determine the best route to overcome driver-error.

While the example may be comically familiar, it is applicable for us in the spiritual journey. Think about the process of going to an unfamiliar place. Ideally, our initial effort to determine precisely where we will go begins before we get in the car. Before getting behind the wheel, presumably we have our destination clearly in mind, and perhaps we have already begun to explore a number of options to find our way. For example, we might use Google to look up an address or consult multiple mapping applications to compare directions. We may call a friend or two who are more familiar with the destination's locale for advice on the best routes. We may even check a news report or smartphone app for traffic problems. That is all part of the effort of calibrating the path from point of origin to our intended journey's end.

What happens, however, when we go off course? Several years ago when my husband and I bought a new home, it was new construction located on a brand new street. The farmhouse that was originally built on the land had been razed, making way for new development. The problem was that ours was the first house built on the new street. So, when I called providers for services such as cable or newspaper delivery, I frequently heard, "There is no such address." It took several months before our street was recognized by the county records and on electronic maps, and I often had to use the old address of the razed farmhouse so others were able to find our home. Using the former address was my consent to recalibrate. I needed a way to help people find me, and modifying the address temporarily became that means.

At times, we all stray from the original route. There are times in life when we think, "If I had only made this decision before, I wouldn't be where I am today." Other times we look back and recognize things have not gone awry, but somehow we have ended up where we always hoped we would be.

Whether we are on track or not, we come to recognize the need to make shifts and changes in our plans if we want to reach our goals. In fact, as we look back, we often realize those changes have made all the difference. This is the process of recalibrating, and the reality of life is that everything needs recalibration from time to time.

Jeremiah understood the need for recalibration. In Jeremiah 10:23, he said, "I know, O Lord, that the way of human beings is not in their control, that mortals as they walk cannot direct their steps." Jeremiah recognized we are not free to direct our own steps. God is in control and only the Lord can direct our steps. However, as we try to exert our will, we find we can too easily get off track. We think we have the right plan or we are heading in the right direction. However, as we run into difficulties or find the path we have taken has not provided us with the outcomes we desired, we realize we need to make a change. It is in recalibrating that we can once again walk the path God has for us.

This is why Jeremiah was asking God to intervene in the recalibration, in a gentle rather than punitive way. He says in verse 24, "Correct me, O LORD, but in just measure; not in your anger, or you will bring me to nothing." If he had to bear God's punishment, Jeremiah recognized he would be brought to nothingness. This is why he asked for God's grace to gently bring things back into alignment.

This is our hope in recalibration: through gentle correction we can be brought back into alignment and not suffer humiliation and embarrassment from failing to follow the course. Recalibration provides such gentle realignment.

The Need to Recalibrate

Recalibration is the practice that allows us to use the work of reflection to see gaps between the work in our current context and our call. It also gives us a chance to discern a strategy (or strategies) to help us regain our footing and get back on track. Considered in this vein, we see the need to recalibrate. It is like checking the directions midway on our journey. We may feel confident we know the way, but sometimes in the midst of the trip we want to make sure we have not made a wrong turn or inadvertently missed our destination.

We check our directions, map, or smartphone to make sure we are still on track. If the way is unfamiliar, we check the route more often so we are more self-assured. None of us want to drive for miles only to find we missed our turn several minutes earlier. I often pull over and consult my resources just to be sure rather than continue to drive with uncertainty. I want to be certain I am still following the path and plan. Such is the need to recalibrate.

This need is particularly vital in ministry. There was clarity of call when I began my pastoral ministry. I knew, or at least thought I knew, what was necessary and how I needed to position my efforts to accomplish the call God had placed on my life. When I heard God say, "Reclaim my church," and recognized I had a specific role in working with youth in the church, I really believed I was to galvanize the young people to help renew the church and her ministries.

My initial plans did not bear fruit in the way I hoped. The children and youth, who I believed were the heart of my ministry, started to fall away from the church. They would participate in a field trip or some outing they thought was interesting, but did not regularly attend Sunday school or worship. That made it difficult to gain any traction as I tried to engage in ministry programming.

Then, my assignment changed. Over the course of eighteen months, I went from being a field education student to associate pastor to senior pastor. I was no longer responsible for only the youth; I was called to lead an entire congregation and that congregation was in decline. Was my assignment still to reclaim the church? If so, what did that mean for my ministry in that time?

I tried to reestablish my church in a community that had seemed to have forgotten we existed. I tried to lessen the deficit-spending situation we were in and to reduce the unsustainable amount of money we were withdrawing annually from our endowment. In addition, I tried to create new energy around a new mission, vision, and programs. These were things I had to do while preaching, teaching, and visiting the sick.

I was doing positive work for the church. However, in hindsight, I am not convinced I was always doing what was necessary in that critical moment. In that season of my ministry, I would have benefited from the practice of recalibrating. Was I still on the path? Was I still following God's plan or had I taken another route, only to find myself meandering along an unnecessary detour?

Many of us have been on that meandering path. A seminarian recounted the decades it took for him to step into his call. He remembered as a child feeling compelled to study and share the Bible with friends and family. Early in life, he felt the stirrings of God's call for him to be a minister, but something happened as he matured. Although others continued to see and acknowledge there was a call on his life, he remained convinced he was to serve God in other ways. He was a youth leader, taught Sunday school, and was active in mission efforts. For him, this work confirmed he was serving God, yet there was restlessness within his spirit.

Years later, someone asked him, "What happened to that call on your life that you felt when you were in high school?" That simple question forced him to recalibrate. In childhood, God placed a call on his life to be a minister. He started out on a path he believed was the right way to go. However, when he looked back, he recognized he had deviated from the path. It was not an intentional divergence. He simply drifted ever so slightly off course and the drifting continued, in his case, for years. When he finally looked back in a kind of review and reconnection, reflection allowed him to acknowledge it was hard for him to identify exactly where he went off track or why. Perhaps he was afraid.

As you remember your call, perhaps you can identify with the experience of fear. I know I was sure God must have made a mistake, that God could not have been calling me. I was terrified by the prospect! Yet, these are times of recalibration, when we are willing to acknowledge the identified disconnections—the gaps that have presented themselves as we reflected on the tasks of our current context and our memories of our call.

When we look at these disconnections, we may find the need to confess we are not where God wanted us to be. We have to do something to get ourselves back on track. In this realization, we are like Jeremiah, who prayed for God's grace in his efforts to redirect his steps. As we humble ourselves, we find that same grace. We become like Daniel, who heard the angel of the Lord say, "Do not fear, Daniel, for from the first day that you set your mind to gain understanding and to humble yourself before your God, your words have been heard, and I have come because of your words" (Daniel 10:12). Recalibration is the practice of setting our mind to discern and gain understanding in humility so we can acknowledge that, perhaps, we have made a wrong turn somewhere along the way.

In time, that young man humbly submitted to God and acknowledged he was following his own path and plan, not God's. It was in this spirit of submission when he realized the need to attend seminary and let go of the false notion that he was called only to lead youth group, Sunday school, or mission projects. Through reflection, God had lovingly reiterated that early call to pastoral ministry. In recalibration, the young man recognized it was time for him to prepare to assume his calling.

When was the last time you rechecked your directions to verify you are still on the right path? Are you where you are supposed to be, or have you been drifting off course?

My son loves jumping waves in the ocean. However, as he plays, he is not always cognizant of what is happening in the ocean current. If you have ever attempted to catch a wave and allow its force to bring you back to shore, you know you drift from your starting position. I have watched my son align himself perfectly in front of my spot on the beach. And I have watched as, with each successive round of riding the waves, he has drifted farther away. The first time he will move two feet, and then six. Within minutes his location will move ten yards or more away from his starting point. Then I find myself standing and waving emphatically to get his attention to return to where he started. Of course, being a child, he is often oblivious to the fact he has moved so far afield.

The same happens to us at times. We don't recognize the slight drift in our life. Sometimes we are so busy doing the work in front of us that we do not look out to the horizon to gauge our course. Sometimes we believe we are doing what needs to be done, never recognizing the tasks in which we are engaged are only preventing us from doing the real work to which we are called. Other times, we engage in work avoidance because the real work—the important work—is too hard or too unfamiliar or too scary. Not knowing where to start, we busy ourselves with what is merely expeditious.

In other words, we drift ever so slightly off course, and if we do not look up to see where we were going, the gap between where we are and where we ought to be continues to widen. We need to stop, look up, and determine whether the current has dragged us down the beach away from where our Divine Parent wants us to be. And if we are off course, we need to recalibrate.

What Is Recalibrating?

What does it mean to recalibrate? How do we know when we have gotten off the path? When I considered the process of recalibrating, I immediately remembered my high-school science experiment. I chose to build a science project that experimented with light. The project used additive color mixing to combine the primary colors of light in an overlapping fashion. By combining red, blue, and green lights in equal parts, I could create white light. However, when colors are added unequally, the result is secondary colors. Thus, when mixing red and green, the resulting color is yellow. When combining green and blue, cyan is produced. When blue and red combine, we see magenta.

Recall how the process of reflection encouraged us to weave together different strands of remembrance. First, we mindfully reviewed the parts and pieces of our current context as the Spirit brought them to our awareness. Second, we reconnected with our call, remembering what God has called us to do. Finally, we reflected on whether our current work is in alignment with our call. Well, as we anticipate the practice of recalibration, let us exchange the analogy of a braided cornrow for the illustration of an experiment in mixing colors of light.

When we are on track, there is no disconnect. Reflection yields the purity of white light. However, when we discover a gap, a secondary color results. The hue may have beauty in its own way, but we know we are not exactly where we want to be. Maybe we have focused too greatly on the current context and lost sight of the overarching goal. Maybe we have focused on the goal to such a degree that we have no means to achieve it because we neglected the infrastructural work required in the current context. Reflection helps us see the disconnects, but recalibration helps us determine the strategies by which we will close the gaps, correct our course, and get back on track.

Thus, recalibration is a process of discernment through which we look at the gaps identified between where we are and where we are called to be and determine how best to realign with God's plan for our lives. It is a process of discernment because we need to be able to see, not only where we have drifted, but also the best strategy for correcting our course.

There are many directions we can take when we find we are off the path, but some strategies yield better results than others. A colleague of mine will often pray for me, asking God to show me when to say yes and when to say no to opportunities, so I may know the difference between what is good and what is best for me. I am notorious for overcommitting and doing too much, even when I am not drawn to the work someone has asked me to do. I can and often do make a good case for doing the many things requested of me. I can always justify something as part of serving others in living out my call as a servant of God. Yet, if I am honest with myself, I know not every opportunity is part of God's plan. In such a moment of humility, I recognize I cannot do it all.

Thankfully, God is faithful, as the prophet Isaiah pointed out to the people of Judah. In Isaiah 30:19-20, God promised to hear our cry and not hide from us. Scripture says, in our humility the teacher appears. As we turn to the right or left, our ears hear a word behind us saying, "This is the way; walk in it." Seeing the illumined path enables us to regain our footing.

How do we get to that path? In Psalm 139, the psalmist acknowledged that wherever we make our bed, God is there. If we ascend to heaven, God is there. If we make our bed in Sheol, God is there as well. This says to me that, regardless of our steps, we will still be in God's abiding presence. That does not mean some of our steps are not better or more effective than others! It is like my colleague praying for my best. How do we determine what is best?

When was the last time you went into a dressing room to try on a new outfit? Like me, you probably turn and strike various poses in the mirror. You want to see how you look from the front, the sides, and the back. Is the fit too tight or too loose? Is the cut flattering? Is the color appealing? These are the questions we ponder in the dressing room. I have been known to take as many as twenty articles of clothing into the small room, only to find none of them fit as well as I would like. That's what the dressing room is for, right? Because, while occasionally we may settle for something less than ideal because of a pressing need, more often we make our purchasing decisions based on what fits best.

Recalibrating gives us the opportunity to try out strategies for our realignment as though we were trying on clothes. We have a number of options to bring ourselves into alignment with where we want to be. But not every path is the best path. Some routes are direct and some are circuitous. In the process of recalibrating, we try to discern the best fit by considering each strategy from every angle, considering complementarity, functionality, comfort, and suitability for the destination. After all, if we were shopping for a planned cruise to Alaska, our purchases would be very different than if our destination were a tropical island!

To return to our original metaphor of recalibration as a kind of spiritual GPS, we need to think through strategies and steps that might reroute us toward our original destination. In our minds we play out how to move and the result of our actions. We try to anticipate whether, having taken certain actions, we will draw closer to the place God has called us to be. In every place where there is a gap, recalibration invites us, as contemplatively as possible, to identify and assess possible strategies for getting back on track. We have to visualize our actions, the result of our actions, and whether our actions will take us where we need to go. As we allow strategies to play out in our mind, we began to see the way and path in which to walk.

Scriptural Grounding for Recalibrating

Jeremiah knew all too well that, left to our own devices, human beings deviate from God's plan. In Jeremiah 10:21, the prophet declared, "The shepherds (religious leaders of Judah) are stupid, and do not inquire of the LORD." Because the leaders failed to consult God in making their plans, they failed to prosper. In verse 23, Jeremiah acknowledged that mortals are incapable of directing their own steps. This is the heart of the Old Testament: the Lord provided the law and sent the prophets to supply direction and help God's meandering people stay on the path.

As people deviate from the divine plan, God extends grace such that, through genuine contrition and a desire to change their ways, the people may be restored. The practice of recalibration makes restoration real. When reflection shows us we are off the path, through recalibration we see a course of correction.

However, recalibration includes the work of discernment. Romans 12:2 says, "Do not be conformed to this world, but be transformed by the renewing of your minds, so that you may discern what is the will of God—what is good and acceptable and perfect." Through review, reconnection, and reflection we experience the renewing of our minds. We see with fresh eyes new directions and new possibilities, rather than being mired in the grip of current challenges. As we rise above the detailed minutia, we are able to discern the will of God.

How Paul defined discernment is critical. He did not want the Roman Christians simply to find the will of God; he wanted them (and by extension us) to identify what is good, acceptable, and perfect. This suggests there is a difference in the options. Some options are better than others, and our desire is to find the best option so we can ensure we are following the best path for our lives.

I am convinced we are also encouraged to explore different options. While I offered the analogy of trying on clothes in a dressing room, the psalmist who penned Psalm 34 used the image of trying a new food. Verse 8 declares, "O taste and see that the LORD is good." The implication is we can try a number of different ways or paths in our effort to find the best way. It is like eating at a buffet where far more food is made available than we can possibly eat. We determine what we will eat by tasting a little bit of many things and then going back for more of what we enjoy most.

We might enjoy everything we try, but inevitably there is one dish we savor above all the others. It is the selection we return to again and again. This is the gift of tasting, be it food or options for pursuing God's call. When we taste, we recognize God's plan for our lives is so much better than anything we might choose for ourselves. God's plan is good and offers us hope and a future (see Jeremiah 29:11). As we taste, we can discern the difference between what is merely good and what is a gourmet dining experience!

As we recalibrate and try different options for getting back on track, we also discern God's presence to guide and direct. By asking, "What is it God wants for me?" we acknowledge we are not left to our devices. God does not want us to go it alone. Psalm 119:105 reminds us that God's word is a lamp to our feet; it illumines our pathway so we know which way to go. As we continue to recalibrate, God continues to direct us. And then, as Isaiah 30:20-21 assures us, God will not hide from us. As our teacher, God is present to help us remain on the path as we intentionally check our directions with the Spirit. As we turn to the right or left, our ears will hear a voice behind us saying, "This is the way; walk in it."

What Pastoral Leaders Say about Recalibrating

A lay leader shared a story with me that serves as a wonderful example of recalibration in the midst of her career ascension. This leader was the executive director of a nonprofit organization, but she faced the challenge of dealing with very difficult board members. She would develop strategic plans and strategies for the organization to share with the board members, but her ideas often met resistance. While a few board members provided a level of support for the new initiatives she tried to implement, there were always staunch holdouts who would block any attempt to change the way things were done.

"I invested so much negative energy into trying to go above and beyond what I was supposed to do to prove something to these people," she admitted. In trying to prove herself, she worked long hours without much satisfaction. Some days she came home absolutely exhausted and disengaged—days when she went straight to bed without interacting with her family. Her family relationships were not the only connections to suffer. Her faith commitment also suffered. She no longer attended the worship services or Bible studies she enjoyed so much. Her job had become so all-encompassing she went to work on Sundays instead of going to church.

This leader finally had to acknowledge she was no longer on the right path. She conceded, "I'm going to work, but people are working against me. I don't have time for that."

She stopped to consider what she wanted to do and what she felt led to do, and then she compared those insights to what she was doing. The disconnect was immediately clear. She realized, "I want to be able to work, to have energy to be able to do what I have to do for the girls that I represent in this organization." Yet, when she considered the reality of her situation, she admitted, "I don't have the energy. I don't have the passion or the desire anymore."

What did this leader finally do? She quit her job. It was a tough transition, but after the separation was complete, she confided that it was the best thing that had ever happened.

In the spiritual practice of recalibration, she thought about her priorities—her family, her faith, and time for herself. With those priorities firmly in mind, she reconnected with her family, which was incredibly energizing for her. Her son had just entered kindergarten, so she was able to volunteer at his school. She also reconnected with her faith community and started attending the women's study group again, having taken nearly a year and a half away because of her crushing job.

These strategies for recalibrating were life-giving. People started saying, "You're a completely different person." But she replied,

"No, ... I'm back to being me. I'm not being the robot and trying to impress anybody. This is who I am."

Having experienced the need for major recalibration, this leader intentionally works to remain on her God-led path. Even in her new job, however, she finds it easy to get caught up in a stressful pace since she works with other managers who can be very intense. At times, she admits, there is the temptation to say, "Oh God, you know, I need to be doing something different." Then she comes back to herself and says, "No, I don't." She is clear about her role and what she is called to do. Recalibrating keeps her on the God-ordained path.

Why Do You Need to Recalibrate?

This leader's story is not much different from ours. Sometimes in our work life we are so focused on what is in front of us that we blindly plow ahead without reflecting on whether those immediate tasks are the right thing to do. Are we doing productive work, or are we avoiding the critical work? These are the times when we have to stop and intentionally recalibrate.

Recalibrating acknowledges the gap recognized during reflection and provides the space to determine how to close the gap to better realize God's best plan for our lives. Recalibration is the necessary midcourse correction that ensures we do not drift too far afield. It is the work of discerning between the better and best so we can follow God's way rather than our own. It is the thoughtful and intentional effort to stay on the path.

What makes recalibrating so difficult? Too often, human nature suggests it is better to do *something* so that we are perceived as productive, even if only by ourselves. Occupying ourselves with busywork can feel productive at times, much more so than the quiet contemplation needed to recalibrate. But what if we took the time to assess the results of our reflection? What if we took the time to consider prayerfully what God has for us to do? In what ways are we not fully living into the call God has placed on our lives?

Such consideration would help us prioritize the work, which in turn will help us recognize what work is most important to accomplish. So much of what we do is not critical to our call. Certainly, we do not have the luxury of ignoring everything that does not fit into our idea of call. Yet, our days would look much different if our work were determined after engaging the practice of recalibration. We may find our busyness dramatically decreases, providing more space to hear God's voice say, "My child, this is the way, walk in it."

What Can You Do to Recalibrate?

I had the opportunity to participate in a "gap analysis" exercise recently. We were encouraged to consider our current state given a specific theme. Asked to reflect on what was going on in the present and how things were working, we then considered the ideal state. Knowing what we knew about our present capabilities and what was possible given emerging technologies, what did we want to see? This was the opportunity to dream a world and a new vision of possibility.

Given this assessment of current and future states, we identified the gaps. What was missing and what was necessary to get us from the present to the future? That gap analysis spoke to the strategy and direction we needed to take. However, the analysis also presented numerous options. Should we invest in new capabilities? Should we expand our operations? Or should we downsize and eliminate aspects of the work from the option set? Each question required different considerations to determine the best path of pursuit.

If reflection serves as the first stage of gap analysis, recalibration is the next step. In review, we see the current work. In reconnection, we remember God's calling and its implications for the future. In the practice of reflection, we weave those views together to contrast present and future states. In recalibrating we assess options, offering them up to God in a process of discernment so we can determine the best way to return to the path God has for us.

So, envision these gaps in your vocational journey—the disconnect between where you are and where God wants you to be. Is there a way to bring what is disconnected into closer alignment? If so, what are the strategies for doing so?

See yourself assigning each strategy a color on the spectrum and project it against the backdrop of God's call on your life. Then begin to mix the strategies as I once mixed colored lights, and see what new color results. As you cycle through the light show, ask, "Is this the shade you had in mind for me, Lord?" Each combination of strategies will produce a different hue, from soft pinks to brilliant oranges to muddy browns. You'll be drawn to some and appalled by others. You may even be suddenly struck like Moses on Mount Horeb or Paul on the Damascus road, blinded by the pure white light of God's perfect plan.

Don't rush the process, however. In fact, try to have fun with the experiment, like a child discovering the joy of mixing watercolors or playing with a prism in the sunlight. Invite God to engage with you in the exploration, exclaiming at each new discovery and asking the Spirit, "What do you think of this one? How do you like me bathed in this color?"

Be present to your feelings as you ask the questions as well. Do you feel drawn to a particular strategy or combination of strategies, or do you shrink away? Does an idea cause you anxiety or give you peace? Taste your own emotional response with each idea that comes to mind. Do not conform to what you think ought to be done. Instead, be transformed as you discern God's desire for you. Know God's plan is good; it gives you hope and a future so you can be fully all that God has called you to be.

In other words, taste and see that the Lord is good. You will know the way to go when you follow a path illumined by God's word and the brilliant light of that ideal-for-you combination of strategies that complement you and spotlight your call. As you recalibrate, you will focus on what is critical and important for now.

So What?

When I consider the results of recalibration, once again I think about the leader who quit her job to get back on course. She told me, after recalibrating, "I was a lot more relaxed."

She laughed as she confessed driving like the stereotypical little old lady after recalibrating. She was no longer in a rush to get anywhere. The realization allowed her to rediscover who she was and where she wanted to be. She liked herself and embraced the pursuit of priorities that were significant. Pleasing others and working exorbitant hours were no longer important to her. Family and church became her main concern when she reprioritized her life through recalibration. She was happier and healthier. Just as important, through recalibrating, she had the ability to offer happiness and health to others.

Questions to Consider

1. Imagine quitting your job to get back on the path and plan God has for you. What does that look like? How do you feel imagining it?

2. When have you come to realize you were no longer on the path God had mapped out for you? What did you do to get back on track?

3. Perhaps, through this chapter, you recognize you have drifted from God's plan. What ideas of recalibration occur to you?

4. What strategies for getting back on track might you try on for size? Has a strategy emerged that you think may be best? Take some time, try some strategies on for size, and write down an action plan to implement recalibration.

·10·

return

The man from whom the demons had gone begged that he might be with him; but Jesus sent him away, saying, "Return to your home, and declare how much God has done for you." (Luke 8:38-39)

WE CAN ONLY imagine the inexpressible joy experienced by the man healed by Jesus. This possessed man had been completely unable to participate in society because of the legion of raging demons that dominated his life. However, at the height of his isolation and estrangement, this man met Jesus, who delivered him of his possession. Feeling grateful, indebted, and committed to Jesus, the man begged to become a disciple. He wanted to be with Jesus wherever he went.

But Jesus said no. He said, "Return to your home." The Gospel of Mark quotes Jesus' words to the man: "Go home to your friends, and tell them how much the Lord has done for you, and what mercy he has shown to you." The man wanted to stay with Jesus, but Jesus told him to return.

The song "In the Garden" expresses the same sentiment. Composer C. Austin Miles saw a vision of Mary Magdalene visiting the empty tomb, where she was the first to encounter the resurrected Christ. The song depicts Mary relishing her time with Christ. She is lost in the moment of simply basking in the Lord. She hears his voice. She walks with him, and they share a precious time of intimate personal conversation. Their time together is so fulfilling and satisfying that Mary does not want it to end, even though the night is falling around her. The song says Jesus "bids her go through a voice of woe." He tells her she must return to a world in need of her gospel ministry.

Through this intentional process of retreat, release, review, reconnect, reflect, and recalibrate, we find sanctuary. Remember, it was Ronald Heifetz who commended sanctuary—the physical or mental space where we can restore our spiritual resources. It is a safe place, removed from the demands and challenges of leadership, a place that offers us the opportunity to consider our challenges, learn lessons, reflect, and regain a sense of purpose, even as we are revitalized. And because this process provides a spacious place for contemplative reflection and recalibration, we gain increased capacity to be effective in leadership. Thus, our time of sanctuary ultimately motivates us to return.

Many of the pastoral leaders I spoke with drove themselves to a time of sanctuary in response to a leadership challenge, just as the demoniac was driven to the tombs by the demons that possessed him. Having engaged in the practice of sanctuary, however, those pastoral leaders emerged with new ideas, strategies, and a readiness to reengage their leadership contexts. They did not want to run away; rather, they wanted to return because they knew what to do differently. They were ready to try again.

This is the step that completes the sanctuary process. We have had an opportunity to step away from leadership to partake in restorative spiritual practices. Having been refreshed, refocused, and renewed, we can get back in the game with our recalibrated strategies in hand. The practice of return gives us the space and grace to do just that.

The Need to Return

The practice of return provides us with a variety of benefits. First, having had the opportunity to identify new ideas or strategies as we recalibrated, return begins with a joyful celebration of our time apart. One year, my church leadership team gave me a gift for my birthday. At the time, it did not feel like a gift because I did not know what it represented. I was merely handed a cryptic note with directions to a location in western Massachusetts.

I distinctly remember the trip. I complained the entire drive: "Where am I going? I don't have time for this. I'm tired and here I am on the road." These were only a few of the grumbling sentiments I expressed along the way. But when I arrived at the destination and checked in, I found my leadership team had given me a spa weekend. I had the entire weekend to retreat, during which I was able to take yoga classes, pray, and meditate. They had made a reservation for me in a lovely bed and breakfast where I ate gourmet meals and received pampering.

It was a glorious time, and I was filled to bursting by the experience. I remember dancing with complete abandon during a class that encouraged us to allow our spirits to soar. As I rested after the dance, I heard the Spirit say, "You are my daughter." I cried tears of joy. It was such a joyous experience that, upon my return, I shared my joy with my congregation. In fact, my experience became the topic of my next sermon, and I twirled on the chancel before the congregation as I relived the joy and included them in it. In the process of return, I experienced joy, and in celebrating that joy, I wanted to share it.

Second, return presents the chance to be grateful for the time apart. When we have desperately needed a break and seized the opportunity to get away, we give thanks for the time apart even as we return. The challenge is to seize the opportunity for gratitude in the same way that we seized the chance to get away!

A pastor described his struggle through a process of guided meditations. The facilitator leading the group encouraged participants to "go deep" to experience the divine. Try as he might, this pastor complained, "I don't get it." He did not feel anything in particular. He did not know what he was supposed to do in the silence, and he was frustrated by the entire experience.

Then the facilitator encouraged him to use the silence to express gratitude for the time. She told him, "Just be grateful." With her suggestion, he was able to appreciate being in the company of other clergy colleagues. He was able to appreciate being away from his desk and the pressures of his work environment. He was able to appreciate the time apart as a time of rest. And from that place of appreciation, he returned to ministry feeling grateful. When we ground ourselves in gratitude, that gratitude becomes a restorative experience that empowers and inspires our return.

Third, the practice of return can fortify us with a sense of affirmation, helping us find strength in times of ministry challenge. In difficult circumstances, dread of what we may find upon return may threaten to deprive us of any sense of gratitude. For example, one pastor, who had been temporarily removed from his pulpit for disciplinary reasons, suffered tremendous embarrassment from the situation. He confessed he wanted to leave his church, but leaving was not so simple. He shared, "I tried to leave, but it was clear that God had not released me. I had to go back."

We saw that dynamic in the story about the demon-possessed man Jesus encountered in the tombs. Upon being restored and delivered, the man desperately wanted to go on with Jesus. Yet, Jesus commanded him to return—return to his home and his family and friends. After experiencing the joy and gratitude of a sanctuary experience, we may crave more—more rest, more reconnection, more time and space to reflect and recalibrate. But more often than not, we will be called on to return—to gather up all we have learned, all we have had restored to us, and go back home. While this may feel disappointing, we can be encouraged by the call to return because we realize God is not finished with us; our ministry continues.

In an even more dramatic way, this troubled pastor wanted to leave the context of his humiliation and grief behind. However, he trusted in God and felt affirmed in the conviction that God had called him to return. Later reinstated as pastor and recognizing God's presence, he set his sights on rebuilding his ministry at the church. Having returned, this leader felt reenergized in his ministry and continued with a renewed sense of strength.

Finally, return is an opportunity to express our eagerness to get back to our ministries. We do so energized with a readiness to reengage in leadership. I met with a seminary professor who was concerned about her theology students. She lamented that they entered her class and immediately launched into complaints and concerns. Their overwhelmingly negative focus made it difficult to help them seek positive resolutions to their challenges.

I listened as she shared, and then I observed aloud that, in our time together, she was doing exactly what she complained her students did. After helping her see herself, we began to discuss strategies she could apply in her classroom to help her students. She identified several approaches and we worked together to refine them. The energy in the room changed as we talked, and she was excited by the thought of returning to her class. She was eager to put the new ideas into practice. Raring to return, she could hardly wait to see her students.

If you have ever had a restorative vacation, you might be able to appreciate these experiences of gratitude, self-affirmation, and renewed energy in your return. Perhaps you actually managed to get away for that time apart with family or friends when no one in the congregation died, no calamities occurred, and you managed to unplug completely from your phone and e-mail. It happens, sometimes!

Being refreshed from the experience of personal sanctuary, you actually felt a readiness to return. When you had time to relax, you discovered new thoughts and ideas rising to the fore. You may have had an epiphany regarding a sermon series or Bible study. You may have gotten an idea about starting a new ministry. The chance to reconnect with your family may inspire in you a more positive outlook and a surge of creative energy for dealing with that persistent ministry challenge back home.

Such experiences create a motivation for return and make our time in sanctuary worthwhile. Whether we feel celebratory, grateful, strengthened, or eager in the return, these outcomes embolden us for continued ministry. We find ourselves wanting to get back. We have new perspective and energy; we feel a renewed sense of well-being and purpose. These feelings prepare us to reengage in our ministry context.

Ministry ebbs and flows. We recognize a need to rest and retreat to realize time apart. But we return so we may continue in our call, inspired and renewed by the Spirit to do the work God has given us to do.

What Does It Mean to Return?

To return means to go back, specifically to our leadership context, refreshed and ready to reengage the work we are called to do. However, like the preceding steps of this process, return encompasses multiple components and a sense of intentionality. To prepare for return, we need to first acknowledge that many feelings may emerge from the opportunity to engage in sanctuary.

Many of the pastoral leaders with whom I spoke experienced wonderfully positive and affirming feelings as a result of their time of sanctuary. Some experienced peace or calm. Some expressed a feeling of ease, as if they had shed a heavy burden. Others said they were relaxed and at one with God.

On the other hand, some expressed the surfacing of difficult feelings as they engaged in sanctuary. One individual described battling with the forces of evil as she worked through personal problems. Another leader spoke of experiencing physical heaviness as a result of evil spirits. For some, taking time apart created a sense of guilt, fearing their time could be better spent doing other things. While we may know differently, these guilty feelings are very much in line with society's message that doing something, even if it is the wrong thing, is better than sitting idly.

Whether the emotions are uplifting or challenging, the first part of the return encourages us to sit with those feelings. We need to give ourselves space to marinate in them and allow those emotional responses to have their full effect. We will want to savor the experience of feeling at rest, at peace, and at one with God. But we may also need to plumb the depth of any negative experiences, to seek God's wisdom and guidance about why we felt guilty or under attack. Do not rush through this part of the process. Take your time, and then allow yourself to experience the gratitude found in making space to feel and experience.

Having had time to discern and process your feelings about the sanctuary experience, you will want to organize yourself for going back. I think of my ritual of returning from a routine business trip. As I begin the process of packing, I check every hotel room drawer to make sure I leave nothing behind. I check the closet to ensure that the sneakers or flip flops packed for down time have made it back into my suitcase. I inventory my clothing to confirm I really have everything.

Preparing to return to our leadership context requires a similar kind of ritual. You may have entered our time of sanctuary contemplating a particular challenge. Do you have some ideas about what you want to do differently when you return? You may have entered the time of sanctuary contemplating your call or your next season in ministry. Do you have a newfound sense of how God is leading? Maybe you entered sanctuary just needing an interval of rest. Do you feel more at peace having taken the time apart?

Preparing for return means inventorying where we are to make sure we have accomplished what we wanted or at least having identified some follow-up activities when we next have the chance to seek a place of sanctuary. Then, we return with a sense of satisfaction.

I remember admonishments I received while in seminary. My advisor constantly told me I was too busy and I needed to engage in self-care to slow my pace and savor the experience. I never made the time. Cognitively, I knew I needed to engage in practices that would be enriching for my spiritual well-being. Still, taking the time seemed to be something I could not afford. But the process of taking time apart to engage in spiritual practices is an essential for leaders, not a luxury. As we have seen, sanctuary promotes and enhances greater effectiveness in our ministerial leadership.

This is not to say finding sanctuary—taking time apart from our leadership context to engage in spiritual practices—is a panacea. All will not be right with the world just because you stepped temporarily off the treadmill. There may be things left undone or an accumulation of items awaiting your return. But because of your time spent in sanctuary, you will be more equipped, energized, and empowered to resume your efforts.

And having taken the time is, itself, worth celebrating. We can celebrate the time apart for the rest we experienced. We can celebrate the ideas and memories we reviewed, reconnected with, and reflected upon. We can celebrate new ideas that may have surfaced. We can celebrate the privilege and blessing of time alone with God. And we can celebrate our commitment to engaging an important practice for our leadership.

We may not feel we have accomplished anything tangible in the time apart. The challenges we faced when we began our period of sanctuary may loom just as large as they were when we started. But we often return with clarity, ideas, and plans for how we will reset and start anew. And we can return with gratitude, if nothing else— a heart full of gratitude for the moments of respite.

Scriptural Grounding for Return

Considering the concept of return and recognizing the potential for ambivalent feelings associated with our return, I think Genesis 16 offers a biblical model for this seventh step of the spiritual practices of sanctuary. In this passage, Sarai has given her slave, Hagar, to her husband, Abram, because Sarai herself was barren. Sarai hoped that Hagar might provide the son and heir that she and Abram longed for.

However, once Hagar conceived, she became haughty toward Sarai. This attitude angered Sarai, and she complained to Abram. He told Sarai that Hagar was subject to her; thus, Sarai had authority to do as she wished. Scripture tells us Sarai dealt harshly with Hagar, which caused Hagar to run away.

An exiled and despairing Hagar sat near a spring in the wilderness when the angel of the Lord found her and inquired about her situation. When Hagar admitted she had run away, the Lord told her to return to her mistress (v. 9). This directive must have created panic in Hagar because she had been abused by Sarai, possibly beaten and subjected to humiliating treatment. How could God expect her to go back to that environment?

When the Lord told Hagar to return, however, God also made a promise to her—a promise that would sustain her in the challenges to come, a promise that would bear her up and strengthen her. The Lord told her in verse 10, "I will so greatly multiply your offspring that they cannot be counted for multitude." The angel went on to tell Hagar she would bear a son to be called Ishmael, which means "God hears." Then, Hagar ventured to name the God whom she encounters El Roi, which means "the God who sees."

God saw and heard Hagar's situation and interceded in a way to make it possible for her to return. The angelic encounter gave her the hope and strength she needed to follow the Lord's command and return.

In sanctuary, we have the opportunity to encounter God as Hagar did. She was in the wilderness—a place to which we can relate as we consider some of the challenges of leadership, and yet she was near a stream—waters that can represent God as our sustaining source and supply. So, connected to that source, we recognize God sees and hears us in the midst of our time apart. Moreover, God gives us what we need to return to our leadership context ready to face the challenges that may have confounded us. This is why we can go back: God has prepared the way for us to return.

The same spirit is reflected in Exodus 4:19, where God says to Moses, "Go back to Egypt; for all of those who were seeking your life are dead." Interestingly, in the passages preceding this word from the Lord, Moses pleaded with God to send someone else in his stead. He expressed concern that people would not believe God had sent him, nor listen to what he had to say. Moses objected that he was not eloquent of speech (perhaps meaning he stuttered). In fact, Moses continued to offer objections until God became angry with him.

Ultimately, however, a change happened in Moses. He submitted to God, recognizing the assignment was his. In his submission, Moses was able to ask his father-in-law to release him so he could return to Egypt. This is what happens to us in the process of returning, as well. We receive confirmation of our assignment and we prepare to go forth to engage the assignment, whether it is something we want to do or not.

Moses certainly did not want to go back to Egypt. In addition to the objections he voiced to God, we also know he was a wanted man, having fled Egypt a murderer. However, something happens as we submit to the need to return. God gives us the assurance to make it possible to return. God prepares the path and makes it safe to return. That is not to say the assignment will be easy. On the contrary, Moses learned en route to Egypt that God would intentionally harden the heart of Pharaoh, making Moses' task all the more difficult. Yet, the knowledge and awareness remained that God was with Moses, and as a result, Moses could return.

In the New Testament, we have another biblical model for return in the narrative of the healed demoniac, where this chapter began. Luke's Gospel does not tell us how the man felt about his denied request. I can imagine him being disappointed. It is understandable the man wanted to follow Jesus out of gratitude for his healing. But, given the infamy of the man's situation under the influence of demons, it is also conceivable he just wanted to go anywhere he could be anonymous. However, the text reflects neither of these sentiments. And, following Jesus' command, not only did the man return home to tell his friends about the goodness of God, but he went to the Decapolis to share the good news about his healing there, too.

While we know there is a historic location called the Decapolis, the city's name also seems symbolic of the man's work. He had instructions to go to his own home to share the news, but he did ten times more than Jesus asked. He did not simply go to his polis, his city. He went to the ten cities—the Decapolis—where he amazed all who heard his testimony.

How was it possible for this man to be such an on-fire evangelist for the gospel? It was the result of his healing—Christ had delivered him from a demon legion and restored him to his right mind. Having had this amazing encounter, the man knew who he was. He knew his purpose and mission. He knew what needed to be done. He needed to return. And in returning, he was not content to share his story only with family and friends. He had boundless energy to go beyond and extend the blessing he had been given.

This is evidence of God's spirit in action. God gives us the ability to do the work to which we have been called and prepares us as we return to ministry.

What Do Pastoral Leaders Say about Returning?

As pastoral leaders spoke of returning to their leadership context, they did not limit their thoughts to this single component of the 7 Rs process. Rather, they spoke inclusively of having engaged in larger sanctuary experience, and then described what it felt like to return from that time apart. The results were dramatic in many ways.

One leader said the experience "changed the way I understood my role as bishop." During her time of sanctuary, she had engaged in praying with the resurrection and the movement out into the world from the resurrection. Specifically, she prayed with John 21, which features a dialogue between Jesus and Peter. Jesus asked Peter three times whether Peter loved him. When Peter responded repeatedly, "Yes, I love you," Jesus said to him in turn, "Then, feed my lambs . . . Tend my sheep . . . Feed my sheep."

As this pastoral leader prayed these passages, she heard specifics about how to operate in her role as bishop when she returned. She completely changed her model of leadership upon her return. For example, in semiannual supervision reviews, instead of asking her staff how they had fulfilled their goals, her first questions became, "How is your spiritual life? How is it with you and God?" Having returned from a time of sanctuary, she came to appreciate more deeply how a person's spiritual well-being affects the rest of life.

Yet, for this bishop the sanctuary experience also had its challenges. She observed that during sanctuary her time of prayer took her to such depths of consciousness and unconsciousness she sometimes had sleepless nights. She had to do battle with what she called the powers of darkness, wrestling with internal questions and sorting through various things. These times were stressful. However, as she moved toward the end of her time apart and prepared to return, she experienced peacefulness as well as an eagerness to get back to her call.

Another pastoral leader, a missionary, also spoke of the experience of sanctuary changing her leadership style upon her return. This Harvard-educated leader and academic spoke of always wanting to reference sources to increase her credibility as she worked with others. However, as she engaged in sanctuary, she gained confidence and boldness in her spiritual gifting and not merely in her academic training. She possessed the gift of knowledge such that she had a God-given sense of what was happening or going to happen in someone's life. Because many people did not understand her gift, she had been hesitant to share it or talk about it. Instead, she chose to speak from her academic credentialing rather than from the knowledge given by the Spirit. Having returned from the experiences of sanctuary, she speaks now from what God gives her when she counsels others. This has had a transforming effect on her ministry and leadership.

Another pastor, when asked what changes he experienced upon return from sanctuary, said, "I am less impatient." Upon return, he has discovered an increased capacity for creativity and wisdom in decision making. He comes out of a more authentic space—not necessarily the space others want him in, but rather where he wants to be. The experience of sanctuary made him more comfortable with his work upon return.

These experiences characterize the results of return, having engaged in sanctuary. We gain a better sense of our work so we return with greater clarity about what we are to do. We gain a greater sense of God's gifting in our lives. Encountering God in sanctuary gives us boldness such that we can live fully into who we are and who we are called to be. This enables us to minister authentically to others, making us more effective leaders because we are fully and freely ourselves.

Why Do You Need to Return?

During my corporate career I experienced a period when I struggled to advance. I was constantly under the leadership of supervisors with whom I had conflicts. Being impatient, I changed organizations and, at times, changed jobs just to get away from what I deemed to be unreasonable or untenable management relationships. However, I began to recognize a pattern. No matter how many times I made such changes, I found myself in the same type of supervisory relationship.

Over time, I came to understand the cycle was repeating because God was trying to help me learn something about myself. Rather than learn the lesson, I kept trying to jump ship, hoping avoidance would help me to maneuver around the challenge. It was not until I stayed in the situation and learned what I needed to learn about working with these senior managers that I was able to move on and move forward.

What I did not understand was this need to return. Feeling the pain was too great and I wanted out, but without the crucial learning, I was bound to repeat the same patterns that were causing my problems. Rather than try to escape, I needed to submit and learn what it was I was supposed to do and how I was supposed to work differently.

While I did not name it as such at the time, I had to engage in a process of sanctuary. I needed time apart to understand where I was in my leadership and what I needed to do. Having had that time to take stock of where I was, I was able to return with a new commitment to learning what I needed to advance in my career.

I realized that, like Hagar with Sarai, I needed to submit to managers who were senior to me. I needed to learn the lesson of *fol-low*ship—following the leader—so that when I became the leader, I was able to be someone others would want to follow. Learning this lesson allowed me to return and be a better employee. More than that, learning the lesson allowed me to return and advance to become a senior leader in the organization.

We are no different in ministry. We need times of sanctuary to assess where we are in our ministry. What is going on in our leadership and our call? As we encounter God, how do we experience God's leading? What should we be doing and what strategies or ideas are at our disposal? We gain the benefit of this learning as we prepare to return. We become cognizant of what we should do when we go back and that sense of new (or renewed) awareness prepares us.

Why do you need to return? Maybe in sanctuary you recognized (and satisfied) the need to have time apart with God. Upon your return, you continue practices of retreat, which center you in peace and calm. You have become a more generous and compassionate pastoral leader. Returning from sanctuary enables you to minister from a place of fullness, not depletion.

Maybe in sanctuary you realized you felt hurt and broken in ministry. Upon being asked, "What are these wounds on your chest?" you may have responded in the words of Zechariah 13:6, saying, "The wounds I received in the house of my friends." In sanctuary, you experienced the healing love of God given through Jesus Christ, enabling you to forgive the hurts and acknowledge your love for those who hurt you. From that place of healing, you return filled with a desire to extend compassion so relationships may be restored.

Maybe in sanctuary you realized your assignment was not yet complete; there is more for you to do in your ministry. Time apart, in this instance, becomes an occasion when you can reflect on the identified gaps, take inventory of recalibrating strategies, and ready yourself to return with a kit bag filled with ideas of what to do and when to do it.

Maybe in sanctuary you recognize you have completed the work you were called to do. Remember the pastor who had a sense her work was done? Not until she prepared to return did she experience confirmation that God's guiding cloud had moved; she also found the strength to inform her congregation she was resigning. Upon return, this pastor was able to leave her position to prepare for the next chapter of her ministry.

Returning gives us the opportunity to assess where we are after sanctuary. Then we can go back to our leadership context ready to engage in healthier and more effective ways. It is the intentional step of going back equipped with what we need to be successful. Why do we need to return? Ultimately, we return to do what God is calling us to do.

What Can You Do to Return?

The first order of business is to acknowledge it is time to return. Have you ever watched children jumping rope? I think back to the days when two friends turned the ends of the rope. As the rope loops in a rhythmic pattern, the person preparing to jump in pauses to gauge the timing of the rope's circular motion. Jumping in too soon or too late causes the jumper to tangle in the line. Instead, the jumper leans in ever so slightly, watches the rope turn, and then determines the precise time to jump in, just as the rope reaches its turning apex.

In the same fashion, we have to prepare to return. The practice is not as simple as declaring, "That was nice," standing from our seated location, and going back to our offices. We have to acknowledge there was a time and space in which we had the privilege to engage.

A denominational leader once complained to me that he was so busy he was not able to take a break during the day. He sat in his office and stared at his computer for hours because there was so much to do.

This is often our narrative in pastoral ministry. The busyness is overwhelming, and it requires self-discipline to break away from the frenetic activity to engage in intentional spiritual practice. When we *have* exercised the discipline to participate in a time of sanctuary, the last thing we want to do is short-change the experience by having it end too abruptly. Rather, we need to acknowledge we have had this time apart and be thankful for the opportunity. We need an attitude of gratitude whereby we say, "Thank you, Lord, for helping me make this time a priority just to be in sanctuary with you."

Then, we need to take stock of what we heard from the Lord or learned about ourselves while in sanctuary. I have a spiritual practice that involves sitting in an isolated room to pray and listen for God. After maybe 30 minutes, I reflect on the experience. What did I hear? What I did sense? What did I feel as I listened for God? Because I do not trust my ability to keep these details and feelings straight, I record my reflections in a journal. More than serving as a memory jog, my notes help me see how faithfully the Lord has moved me through various challenges and obstacles. I can see God's faithfulness, grace, and mercy. Moreover, I see my growth and deepening faith as I abide in God. Because my practice usually occurs at the beginning of the day, I often bound out of my guest room ready to take on the world. I have an idea and a plan, and I am ready to return to the routine rhythms of life because I have captured in sanctuary what God has said and how God has moved, making me ready to press on.

This is the point: what you can do to return is get ready. God is preparing you for greater things. So, get ready to go back. Have an emboldened spirit that says, "Here I am, Lord. Send me!"

Get excited whether you have a grand plan or not. In sanctuary, God will give you what you need because you have drawn near to the source of living water that restores the soul.

So What?

Remember the powerful testimony from the bishop who, after returning from sanctuary, said the experience fundamentally changed how she did her job? Having had the privilege of working with seminarians and new ordinands, I know they often experience a changed view of ministry after seminary or field education. Even new pastors may witness their perspectives change as they mature in ministry. But there is something significant about a senior leader who acknowledges the changes in her ministry resulting from time apart. Her revelatory admission has had a profound effect on my own ministry.

But the transforming impact of practicing sanctuary is not a newfound discovery. Through the Gospel narratives, we see how Jesus engaged in ministry. Through time apart before ministry, he was more prepared for ministry. Through time apart after ministry, he was restored from the rigors of ministry. Surely, his leadership was more effective as a result.

Truly that is our desire: to become more effective as ministry leaders. As we take time apart from our leadership contexts to engage in spiritual practices, we become more effective in leadership. The opportunity to *retreat, release, review, reconnect, reflect, recalibrate,* and *return* provides the generative capacity to determine a faithful way forward, having reflected on the actions we have taken or the steps we are prepared to take in the context of our leadership. These are the 7 Rs of Sanctuary, and this is the practice I commend to you for your leadership and to the glory of God.

Questions to Consider

1. Are you ready to return? Why or why not?
2. What have you learned about yourself and your ministry through your time of sanctuary? What will you do differently upon your return? What will remain the same?
3. How do you feel: relaxed and at peace? Excited and energized?
4. What are you looking forward to about your return? What aspects about the return cause you anxiety?
5. In what ways are you like Moses or the formerly demon-possessed man who experienced healing?
6. What other scriptural references bring to mind the idea of return? How might they inform you as you prepare to return?
7. What is most present in your mind as you prepare to return to your leadership context?
8. What thoughts came to mind as you read this chapter?